THE HIVE
AGREEMENTS

BEE WISDOM ON SISTERHOOD, SACRED BELONGING & SUSTAINABILITY

THE OG BEES

SACHA STERLING ARPAIA, AMBER KUILEIMAILANI BONNICI
JENNIFER BROWN, NICOLE FOX

FLOWER *of* LIFE PRESS

The Hive Agreements: Bee Wisdom on Sisterhood, Sacred Belonging & Sustainability

By The OG Bees: Sacha Sterling Arpaia, Amber Kuileimailani Bonnici, Jennifer Brown, Nicole Fox

Published by Flower of Life Press
www.floweroflifepress.com
Jane Scott Ashley, *Publisher*

Cover and Interior Design: Jane Scott Ashley

Library of Congress Control Number: Available upon request.

ISBN: 979-8-9954890-0-9

"*The Hive Agreements* is more than a book—it's an invitation for women to rise together in harmony. In a time of burnout and division, this message is both urgent and essential. Through sisterhood, sacred belonging, and sustainability, the OG Bees offer a powerful path to restoring the health of women—and, in turn, the health of our planet. This is a movement whose time has come."

—JJ Virgin, Nutrition & Fitness Expert, NYT Bestselling Author

"This is a beautiful and timely invitation back to sisterhood. *The Hive Agreements* reminds us that we were never meant to do life alone… and that we are stronger when we rise together. A powerful and important read for women everywhere."

—Natalie Southgate, Founder of Chakradance™

"Through the metaphor of the hive, the OG Bees offer a compelling vision and framework for belonging and leadership that speaks to this moment in women's awakening—illuminating a model rooted in interdependence, stewardship, sisterhood, and shared purpose. This is a timely and nourishing read for women who are creating movements, sisterhoods, or heart-centered businesses. It invites us to lead in ways that regenerate and serves as a beautiful reminder that when women gather in devotion and shared purpose, something far greater than the individual emerges."

—Achintya Miranda Devi, Author, Rose Priestess & Founder of Goddess Rising Mystery School

"*The Hive Agreements* is an exemplary blueprint for a golden age of female relationships. The vivid metaphor of the hive in this context is truly inspirational, making the way forward for women to truly connect and support one another as pure, clear, and sweet as honey."

—Natalia Rose, Author of *Raw Food Detox Diet* and Cleansing Mentor

"The Hive Agreements... invites us, in deeply practical ways, to transform how we show up for ourselves and our sisters. It is part manifesto, part memoir, and part field guide, weaving bee science, personal story, and spiritual practice into a framework for the kind of sisterhood many of us have always longed for but haven't quite known how to build. Healing the sister wound is one of the pillars of a collective better future, and the Hive models the way."

—**Christine Marie Mason,** Author and Founder of Rosebud Woman

"The Hive Agreements speak to a kind of wisdom we deeply need right now, the wisdom of the feminine. They remind us that true strength comes through collaboration, care, intuition, and community, much like the intelligence of the hive itself. At a time when many of us feel chaotic, seeking more connection and meaning, these agreements offer a beautiful pathway back to working, creating, and flourishing together… I love this book and aspire to live by the principles!"

—**Deanna Minich,** MS, PhD, FACN, CNS, IFMCP, Author of *The Rainbow Diet,* Teacher, Artist, Speaker

"This is soul sister medicine for the times. It couldn't be a better time for this paradigm of sisterhood and sustainability. The world needs this sweet honey."

—**Elizabeth Arolyn Walsh,** Soul Guide at Sacred Ground & The Sacred Relationship School

"The Hive Agreements cultivate harmony as a coherent frequency— an atmosphere shaped by how we speak, how we listen, and how we hold one another. This book offers women a shared rhythm as a way to gather in clarity and mutual benefit. The devotion that is woven throughout strengthens relationships, communities, and the Earth herself. May this book travel widely. May its hum be steady. May its wisdom take root."

—**Lavender Grace,** Co-Founder of Bee Bold Alliance, Creator of The Honey Hive of Mendocino & Song Keeper

"*The Hive Agreements* is a powerful invitation for women to remember what many of us have forgotten ... that we were never meant to walk alone. Through the sacred metaphor of the hive, the OG Bees illuminate the path back to sisterhood, belonging, and sustainable living. This book beautifully articulates the truth I've witnessed over a decade of facilitating women's circles: when women gather in conscious collaboration, something ancient and transformative awakens. *The Hive Agreements* is both a remembrance and a roadmap for the future feminine."

—**Tanya Lynn,** Founder of Sistership Circle, Author of *The Art of Leading Circle* and the *Women's Circle Ritual Handbooks*

"In a culture that constantly tells women they are not enough, this book stands firmly and compassionately in another frequency: You are sacred. You belong. You are stronger together. If you are longing for authentic sisterhood, for a place where your humanity and divinity are both welcome, or for a new paradigm of collaboration over competition, *The Hive Agreements* will meet you there. This is not just a book to read. It is a movement to join."

—**Lou Reed, Shaman,** Founder of Energy Medicine, Inc.

"*The Hive Agreements* feel like a remembering. A homecoming.
Not something new, something ancient that my body already knows.
A remembering that harmony isn't something we sit around waiting for. It's something we choose. Over and over again.
The choice to trust ourselves.
The choice to stand beside other women without competition.
The choice to belong without shrinking, without performing, without abandoning who we are.
This is the kind of harmony that changes your life forever."

—**Ayelet Polonsky,** Founder of the Manifestation Method Podcast

"Honey for the heart and soul. What a transmission the bee sisters offer us here: not just a clear pathway out of chaos and into coherence using the ancient wisdom of the hive, but the nitty gritty grounding in how real women can show up in this evolutionary moment."

—**Lisa Schrader,** Founder of Awakening Shakti

"There is a quiet revolution happening—one built not on competition, but on compassion. Not on tearing down, but on lifting up. Like bees, who instinctively protect their hive, care for one another, and create something sweet from even the most difficult seasons, women, too, hold the power to transform the world simply by choosing each other. These pages will stir something within you. They will call you back to your sisters—the ones beside you, the ones who came before you, and the ones yet to find their wings. They will challenge you to show up, to reach back, and to believe that no woman's light diminishes your own. Because here, in this sisterhood, there is room for every voice, every story, every dream. Read this book. Share it. Live it. And then pass it on—because that is exactly what bees do."

—**Rev. Charlene Kussner,** Senior Minister, Center for Spiritual Living Temecula Valley

"From the first pages of *The Hive Agreements,* I could feel there was something special unfolding. I finished it in two sittings, moved by the distinct voices of the four authors and the way they weave the wisdom and medicine of the bees into reflections on sisterhood, belonging, and sustainability. Everything is anchored back to the Divine, which made reading it feel like a true heart-opening experience. It's the kind of book you'll want to buy for yourself— and a few copies for the women you love. You'll hear your heart responding as you read… of course… of course."

—**Anahita Ahura,** Founder of She School & TEDx Speaker

Our Prayer for Harmony

May our bodies, hearts, minds, and spirits be open
To create harmony
Within ourselves,
Each other,
And Our world.

May our buzz begin now—
A quiet, sacred, sovereign sound,
Embracing wholeness,
As all of you is welcome here.

May our buzz grow
As we call in north, east, south, west,
Fire, air, water, earth,
A cohesive blend
To create honey and miracles.

May our buzz harmonize
Honoring choice,
Attuning us to Love,
Interconnection,
Interdependence,
And Cross-pollination.

May it connect us, one heart to another,
Co-creating the frequency of
Harmony for all—
The Way of the Hive.

~Blessed Bee

Contents

The Invitation

Welcome, Bee Sister.

This is your invitation from the bees to return to yourself, to remember you already belong, and to realign with the path of harmony. This book is a collective call to return to the ancient wisdom of the Hive.

The Hive does not work alone.
The Hive collaborates, cross-pollinates, interconnects.
The Hive gathers together.

You are invited to join us on this journey, an experiment in discovering the way of the Hive. Together, we'll weave a vision of sisterhood, sacred belonging, and sustainability.

When you join our movement and link arms with the Bee Sisterhood, you are joining a community of women taking a stand for themselves, other women, and the world.

It is a big mission.

There is a reason you are reading this book at this time.
You have been called.

Our hive is not complete without you.
We hope you'll join us.

Sacha, Amber, Jennifer, Nicole
~The OG Bees

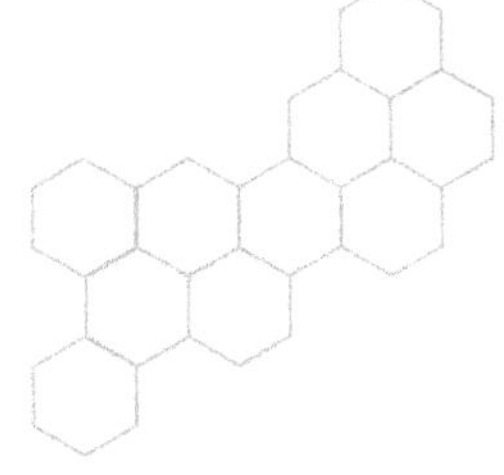

In the Hive, we choose:

Harmony: A coherent frequency of love where we honor truth and expression for ourselves, others, and our world.

Harmony is the Heart of the Hive.

We create harmony through:

- **Sisterhood:** A loving, mutually beneficial relationship between two or more women that honors and respects each other's choices—no matter what.
- **Sacred Belonging:** Acceptance without conditions from the Divine, yourself, and others.
- **Sustainability:** Choosing actions to live in harmony with ourselves, others, and our world.

Introduction ~ The Way of the Hive

No more do we choose me *or* you,
We choose me *and* you.

We are for you.
We are you.
We take up our space.
We build each other up.
We already belong.
We choose community.
We stand together.
We create together.
We cross-pollinate.
We choose more than enough.
We honor our own guidance.

We choose sisterhood, sacred belonging, and sustainability.
We choose the Way of the Hive.

No more do we choose one way *or* another,
We choose one way *and* another.

We choose harmony.
This is a global reset.

Bee Fact: Choice

Forager bees have the autonomy to choose which flowers to visit. Even when shown waggle dances pointing to a specific location, individual bees assess whether to follow the suggestion or seek nectar elsewhere. Their choices are informed by personal experience and instinct, not command.[2]

CHOICE

Before we begin, we must speak about choice.
Choice is the foundation for our work.

You can choose sisterhood.
You can choose sacred belonging.
You can choose sustainability.

You are not required to have these things.
You are not lacking without them.
We are giving you an alternative to what you may have been choosing up until now.

---

2 Grüter, C., & Ratnieks, F. L. W. (2011). Flower constancy in insect pollinators: Adaptive foraging behaviour or cognitive limitation? Communicative & Integrative Biology, 4(6), 633–636.

Your power lives in your choice. There are no agreements without acknowledging you have a choice.

We acknowledge that not everyone's circumstances are the same. This invitation may not serve you or your life at this time.

We acknowledge this is your choice.

Bee Sisterhood is our choice.
And we invite you to join us.

All Are Welcome

The Bee Sisterhood does not subscribe to any one culture or tradition. Bees have been revered for millennia and found across virtually every continent. They have been found in numerous religions and cultures, including Africa, Australia, Native America, China, Japan, Europe, and South America.

For thousands of years, people around the world have both learned from and honored the bees. We continue this tradition.

The Bee Sisterhood does not follow any specific faith or religious tradition.

All faiths and beliefs are welcome in our Hive. Throughout this book, we will refer to the "Divine"—a grace bigger than ourselves. You may call it Source, God, Goddess, Allah, Yahweh, Jesus, Universe, Great Spirit, Buddha, Nature... There are lots of ways people have connected to and honored this energy throughout time.

Please feel free to substitute the word that best fits you.

We welcome all political views, races, socio-economic backgrounds, sexual orientations, ages, abilities, and neurodiversity.

We do not choose sides.

We stand for harmony.

Bee Fact: All Are Welcome

Inside the hive, bees from different roles, ages, and duties interact fluidly, without hierarchy or exclusion. A young nurse, a middle-aged builder, and an elder forager may cross paths, share food, or groom each other. Bees don't judge or divide by status or behavior. They respond to need, not identity.[3]

---

3 Winston, Mark. *The Biology of the Honey Bee.* Harvard University Press. Cambridge, Massachusetts. 1987. 90-101.

Note:
We do not claim to be experts on bees.
We have been called to share this message from the Hive.

PART 1 ~
ABOUT THE HIVE

WHAT IS THE HIVE?

The Hive is a community of women, also known as the Bee Sisterhood, committed to personal growth while working *together* in sisterhood to create harmony for ourselves, each other, and the world.

We cannot do this alone.

The Bee Sisterhood invites and inspires women onto the path of harmony through sisterhood, sacred belonging, and sustainability. We align with bee wisdom while following our hive agreements to guide us as a collective group.

Our vision is that every woman creates a sustainable life, so we create a sustainable world through sisterhood and sacred belonging.

We know when we empower ourselves as individual women, all beings benefit. As we individually change, we change the world.

Bee Fact: Harmony

Hive temperature is kept stable by coordinated wing fanning and shivering. The bees act in precise harmony to maintain a life-supporting environment for the brood.[4]

4 Heinrich, Bernd. *Winter World: The Ingenuity of Animal Survival.* Harper-Bollins Publishers, Inc. New York, NY. 2003. 281.

Harmony

Harmony is the core of our movement. First, we must recognize that harmony is truly possible. Nature, and especially the bees, have already shown us how.

In a beehive, there is order, structure, and cooperation. The hive functions as one, operating on the principle of harmony. We choose to do the same.

A reminder of our definition of Harmony:

Harmony: A coherent frequency of love where we honor truth and expression—for ourselves, for others, and for the world.

Within this definition lies a practice of acceptance and respect. Notice, however, that harmony does *not* require agreement. We can live in harmony while holding different perspectives. What matters most is giving each other space to feel, express, and be, without trying to change one another.

Each of us carries a unique frequency shaped by different life experiences and ways of seeing the world. Expecting everyone to agree is not only unrealistic, it is a disservice to the Divine and to our individual paths.

What *is* realistic, and deeply needed, is the ability for multiple truths to coexist and be honored. When we embrace this, we foster a world where people feel safe to share their hearts, experiences, and ideas. We release the need to be "right," making others "wrong."

The first step to bring harmony is having the courage and willingness to live in our own truth. To believe that our voice, our experience, and our frequency are *necessary* in this world, just as each bee is essential to its hive.

As women, many of us have been taught to seek external validation and guidance. This can disconnect us from our inner knowing and create disharmony within ourselves, and by extension, with others. True harmony begins by reclaiming our trust in ourselves and in our direct connection to the Divine.

Harmony within yourself is the sacred alignment between your inner truth and your outer expression. It's when your energy, emotions, and actions move with your soul's knowing.

It takes courage to be different, to share a perspective that doesn't align with the majority, to express ourselves differently. But if we *don't* do this, if we try to mold ourselves to fit in, we generate dissonance—within and around us.

Imagine how we might engage with one another if we *trusted ourselves*, lived our *truths*, and believed that everyone had access to their own sacred guidance. What if we truly accepted that *our* way is not *the* way for everyone? That each path, while different, may be equally divine?

Can we have the courage to allow others to walk their own path, even when we don't agree?

Can we honor those who see the world differently?

Can we give space for others to share their hearts, even when what they say contrasts with what we believe?

Harmony does not always feel good. Harmony is not the absence of tension, but the presence of coherence. A felt sense that everything belongs—even the contrast. It's the resonance that arises when we start listening.

Harmony takes us out of the conversation of masculine/feminine, liberal/conservative, either/or, and instead brings us into the *both-and.*

Harmony pulls us together rather than separates us.
It is our path to sustainability.

This is our vision, the invitation, the experiment.

Bee Fact: Hive Order

Bees operate on a clear age-based labor system: young bees clean and nurse, middle-aged bees build and guard, and older bees forage. This order ensures the hive functions seamlessly.[5]

5 Johnson, Brian. (2010). Division of labor in honeybees: form, function, and proximate mechanisms. Behavioral ecology and sociobiology. 64. 305-316. 305.

HIVE ORDER

In the Hive, there is a sacred order to things:

#1 Queen Bee—The Divine

The most important part of the hive is the Queen Bee. The bees know she is their top priority. Without the queen, the hive dies. In this Hive, our Queen Bee is the Divine. Our connection with the Divine is top priority.

#2 Individual Bee—Self

Next in importance is the bee itself. If it isn't healthy, it can't contribute to the hive. In the hive, individual bees have choice and trust their instincts to care for themselves. In this Hive, we focus on the sustainability of each woman. When she lives sustainably, she has the energy for herself as well as the overflow to contribute to the Hive.

#3 The Hive—Others

After the Queen Bee is cared for and after the individual bees are healthy and nourished, the Hive collaborates as one. The bees share one goal, as do we. In our Hive, our goal is harmony. When we are connected first with the Divine, our Queen Bee, and then are living sustainably, we have the energy and resources to join forces with others, creating more impact than we ever could on our own.

Bee Fact: Synarchy

During swarming, scout bees democratically choose the next hive location. They vote by dancing, and only when a quorum is reached does the swarm move.[6]

SYNARCHY

Within the hive, the bees embody "synarchy," also known as joint rule or joint sovereignty. This demonstrates how each person operates within their own power and sovereignty, yet chooses to collaborate harmoniously with others. This collaboration isn't just about coexisting but is also about leveraging the unique gifts of each member to support the hive.

The hive doesn't use hierarchical structures that stifle creativity and suppress voices. Synarchy within the Hive means recognizing each woman's individual strengths and sovereignty and creating spaces where these can be expressed and celebrated. In the hive, every bee thrives because the success of one is linked to the success of all. It is the same for us.

---

6 Seeley, Thomas D. *Honeybee Democracy.* Princeton University Press. Princeton, New Jersey. 2010. 135.

Bee Fact: Interconnection

Bees communicate through subtle vibrations that travel across the honeycomb. These vibrations share information about danger, hunger, or changes in hive conditions, instantly connecting the entire colony, even across distance.[7]

INTERCONNECTION

When you look at nature, you can see a variety of ways we have been designed to interconnect. The roots of redwood trees in a grove connect with one another. Mushroom and mycelium underground superhighways transfer information to each other. Trees communicate with each other from miles and miles away, alerting other trees to the danger of a fungus or disease.

The hive is built on the principle of interconnection. No one bee does it alone. It is meant to interconnect, and each bee has its own job and purpose. It's the same in our Hive. We know we have been designed to interconnect.

---

7 Holldobler, Bert & E.O. Wilson. *The Superorganism: The Beauty, Elegance, and Strangeness of Insect Societies.* W.W. Norton & Company. New York, NY. 2009.

Bee Fact: Interdependence

No single bee performs all the tasks needed for survival. Foragers rely on nurses to raise the brood. Nurses need builders to create comb. Builders rely on guards for protection. The hive functions only because each bee depends on the work of the others.[8]

INTERDEPENDENCE

The fastest way for a bee to die is to leave the hive and attempt to survive alone. This looks like many women today—an independent hive of one. If this is working for you, great. If not, *inter*dependence is our way to sustainability.

The bees value cooperation over competition, supporting each other's roles and collectively responding to threats. By doing the same, we can create environments where we do not feel the pressure to "do it all" but can thrive together. This approach is better for the individual and for the hive.

---

8 Winston, Mark. *The Biology of the Honey Bee*. Harvard University Press. Cambridge, Massachusetts. 1987.

Bee Fact: Queen Bee First

Even in the peaceful world of the hive, a colony will descend into conflict if the queen dies suddenly. It will dwindle and die and as it declines, without a queen, the worker bees become highly aggressive towards each other.[9]

THE DIVINE (QUEEN BEE) IS #1

Without the Queen Bee, there is no hive. The queen is number one, before any one bee, before the hive. She is the sustenance and brings life and vitality to the hive.

The primary role of the queen bee is reproduction. She is the only bee in the hive capable of laying fertilized eggs, which develop into worker bees and new queen bees. She can lay hundreds or even thousands of eggs per day. She gives off pheromones that influence the behavior and physiology of other bees to suppress aggression and promote harmony and organization within the hive.

The queen bee is vital for the stability and productivity of the hive.

---

9 Winston, Mark L. *Bee Time: Lessons from the Hive*. Harvard University Press. Cambridge, Massachusetts. 2014.

It is the same with us. When we look at the health of our hive, we must rely on our Queen Bee. Our Queen Bee is the Divine. Without connecting to the Divine, to life force, there is no sustainability, connection, or healing. Our relationship with the Divine serves as the foundation for everything we do.

If you try to help the planet, heal others, or make a difference, and you are not connected to the Divine, it is like trying to drive a car without gasoline, trying to light a fire with no spark, or trying to nourish a baby with no milk.

Here in the Hive, we put first things first. And first things first means prioritizing our connection with the Divine, the Queen Bee.

Everyone does that differently. However you do it is your choice.

A hive is not built by accident. Every bee has a purpose. Each of us did not simply stumble upon this path; we were called. With their ancient wisdom, the bees chose us and guided us here. This is our story—the story of how we answered the call.

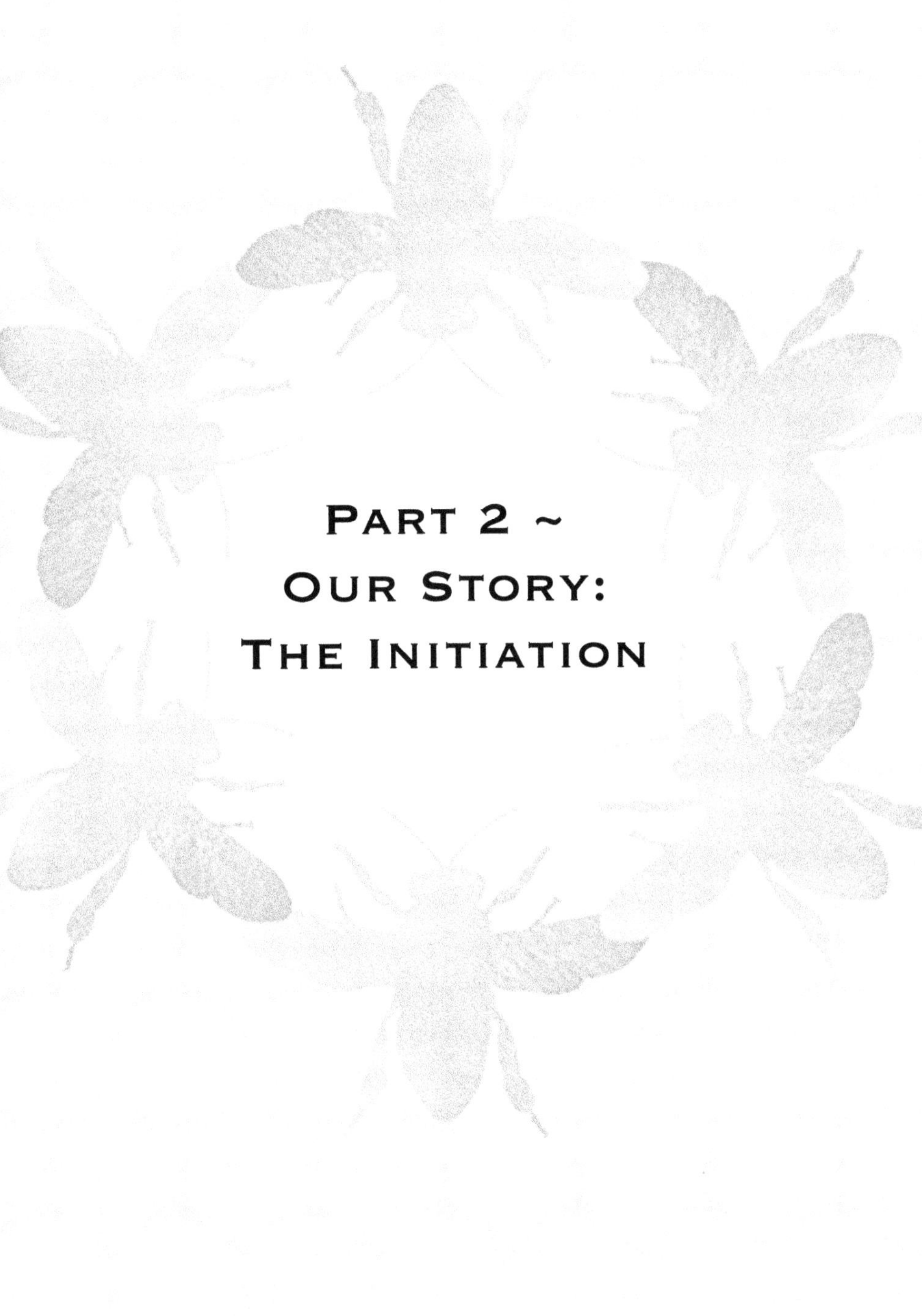

Part 2 ~
Our Story:
The Initiation

The bees came to us when we needed them most. Each of us, in our own unique way, was feeling the strain of living an unsustainable life.

AMBER'S STORY

I was in a dark night of the soul. My grandmother had just died, and I turned 42—the same age my mother was when she died. Financially, after years of building, my company was losing money. It felt like I was being sucked dry.

I felt a deep dissatisfaction with life and was questioning everything. Why was I here? What was the point of everything, all the work, all the effort? I didn't see the point any longer, and looking ahead, it felt like life was just decades of doing the same thing again and again and again.

I needed a change.

Around that time, I was invited to a retreat. During that night, at one point, the four of us, myself, Nicole, Sacha, and Jennifer, found ourselves sitting in a circle with two others. Looking around our circle, I felt the Divine power of interconnection.

Suddenly, instead of sitting in a circle, I saw the six of us, and I thought *six, hexagon, hive, bees*. I felt the energy of interconnection, the possibility of cross-pollination. I felt pulled towards the center of the circle and leaned in. And from deep within, I started buzzing, and one by one, all of us in the circle joined.

As we buzzed, something changed within me. As I looked around that circle and met each woman's eyes, I realized the only thing that had been holding me back from true sisterhood all these years was my own belief that it wasn't available. I knew at that moment that my life would never be the same. And it hasn't.

I believe the bees came to initiate us in the way of the Hive. Ever since, we have been claimed and chosen by the bees.

After that, the four of us stayed connected. We started sharing our lives and deepest pains. We became the Bee Sisterhood, the four of us the OG Bees, and as the years passed, the bees shared what we now call the Hive Agreements—lessons and wisdom from the bees on how to live a life of sisterhood, sacred belonging, and sustainability.

At that point, we realized that the bees' teachings and what we were learning were not for us alone but for every woman. Our Hive was meant to grow.

NICOLE'S STORY

It was a confusing time in my life, and I was in a deep internal struggle. Although I had so much to be grateful for, I couldn't seem to accept all the blessings in my life. Nothing was bringing me joy.

The world felt unsafe. Covid had just happened, I was a mother of young twins, had two businesses, was in my 10th year of marriage, and was feeling very disconnected. I was wearing multiple masks, putting everyone's needs and opinions above my own, and burning the candle at both ends. I was alone, uncomfortable in my own skin, and definitely not living a sustainable life.

A friend wanted to host a retreat and asked me if we could do it at my home. This felt like a blessing in disguise. Around 15-20 people attended, and most were new faces.

The first thing I noticed was that a large majority of these people, mainly women, seemed so powerful and what I would now call very embodied. They felt like they had a strong sense of themselves and were radiating so much beauty and strength. Honestly, I was jealous. I wanted this for myself, and I just felt like they all had something I didn't.

My first response was to put up a big wall around myself and go into a state of comparison. I told myself stories about how I was doing better than them just to make myself feel better.

I told myself they lacked substance or heart. I could only tell myself this for a very short period because it clearly wasn't the truth. The love and commitment they had for themselves and others was calling me forward to look at myself.

I felt a sense of discomfort and sadness, as if I wasn't feeling enough, and a complete emptiness inside. I watched one of the women dance and play with such freedom and thought, "If only I could be more like her."

Looking back, I can see this was my usual pattern—I would either cut women down to boost my own confidence or, if that didn't work, I'd put them on a pedestal, making them seem better than me just to maintain the familiar sense of separation. This would also feed into the "I am not good enough" story, which always seemed to be playing in the background.

During the night, I ended up in the circle that Amber spoke of when we gathered as a hive of women and started to buzz. At the time, I didn't realize what was happening, and I had no idea that this moment would change my life. God was intervening in the pattern I was creating for myself, which was causing my whole life to feel like it was crumbling in front of me. I was given a gift of sisterhood, which we call the Hive, that, in all honesty, has taken me many years to process, integrate, and grow from.

I was given this gift, and I am now ready to share it with all of you. I believe this is not something that will change you overnight, but rather a commitment to yourself and a journey that will ultimately transform your life.

SACHA'S STORY

I was running on the fumes of eternal optimism as both a sincere part of my nature and a coping mechanism. I flew down to this retreat on the recommendation of a friend who could clearly see that I needed something to change. As much as I was trying to keep my life and world together, beautiful, and abundant for myself and my young daughters, my internal world was devastated.

The shock of my father's suicide had changed me permanently, and my initiation with grief was undeniable. I was pretty convinced my marriage was ending, and as a serial entrepreneur with a lot of responsibility, I didn't know when or where I could fall apart.

I had people in my life who loved me and who I loved, yet there were places where I kept myself separate and closed off. Many of my desires for success were fueled by my deeper desire for love and connection. My internal dialogue was saying, "When I'm more successful, have it all together, have reached that important milestone, then I'll be worthy of the unconditional love, intimacy, and support that would feel so good."

I went into this retreat with no conscious expectations—it felt very outside of my comfort zone to prioritize the time and money for something not work or family-related with all that was going on. But thank the Goddess I followed my inner knowing and showed up for life, allowing it to surprise me and for destiny to align.

It was a moment of grace that brought us all together, touching foreheads and buzzing, gazing into each other's eyes, smiling. The light that emanated from each of us as we circled, being moved by the frequency of bee wisdom, was instantly life-changing. A reset. A healing. An invitation. A new tool and way of engaging with life.

The unfolding magic continues to delight me all these years later. The bees want us to experience heaven on earth and share the wisdom and possibility with humanity so that we can create sustainable lives and a sustainable world. Letting go of perceived control to allow a more aligned, collaborative, and authentic version to emerge takes so much courage… courage that is only accessible with sisters we can trust—a hive we can count on.

JENNIFER'S STORY

I had my life set up. My work as a hairstylist was going well, and I was creating more space to do my inner work. Then the pandemic came, and my world fell apart. Everything I had worked for was erased. It was like I had put together a beautiful puzzle that was suddenly pushed off the table into pieces. I felt hopeless, stressed, and consumed with my own depression. I knew I needed support and change, but I didn't know how to find it on my own.

At that same time, I remember walking through the door of the retreat and being welcomed with hugs. The world was telling us that gathering in community was not safe, but all I craved was community and the supportive love that comes through touch. I had never met some of these women and had no idea what impact they would have on my life.

As the retreat progressed, I was in a deep meditation on my own.

I opened my eyes and found a few more eyes finding me. Like magnets being drawn together, we joined in a circle. All of our eyes met. We saw beyond the physical into the depths of our souls, like we had known each other for lifetimes.

We began to buzz. Our foreheads touched. The buzzing changed our vibration. We were called into a higher vibration.

Weeks after the retreat, I recall Amber being the first to suggest that there was something here for the four of us to continue connecting. It was not totally clear at first. We took turns calling each other. We began to meet consistently to deepen our sisterhood. Through this process, we started to redefine what sisterhood meant. We all shared a dream of deep friendship and had not yet fully experienced it in our lives.

We became the Bee Sisterhood. This sisterhood made it possible for me to accept where I was on my journey from a non-judgmental space. They witnessed me in my sadness and grief around childhood sexual trauma and deeply seated self-hatred. The healing came when I was able to be witnessed in my wholeness in whatever stage I was in. I could be in celebration or shame, and I was still seen as whole.

This sisterhood has taught me how to show up for others without sacrificing myself in the process—to support and be fully supported. They gave me a safe place to find my voice and express it. Like me, when you step into bee sisterhood, it is possible to find the lost pieces of yourself, to know and honor your wholeness as a human while celebrating your deep divinity as a woman during this potent time on earth.

Our journeys are different, yet what we have in common is a shared purpose, a calling deeper than any one of us alone. The bees did not just choose us; they entrusted us with a mission.

Part 3 ~
Our Mission:
Sisterhood, Sacred Belonging & Sustainability

At Bee Sisterhood, our mission is that every woman creates a sustainable life—so we can create a sustainable world—through sisterhood and sacred belonging.

We refer to this foundational approach as our "Holy TriniBee: Sisterhood, Sacred Belonging, and Sustainability." These three pillars are the heart of our mission to create harmony.

Choosing sisterhood, sacred belonging, and sustainability is an act of social change, a collective approach to living, leading, and loving. By joining the Bee Sisterhood Movement, you become part of a community of women who choose themselves, other women, and the planet.

Bee Fact: Sisterhood

Honey bee colonies are made up almost entirely of sisters—female worker bees who all come from the same mother (the queen). These sisters cooperate in foraging, raising young, cleaning, and protecting the hive. Their unity and collaboration form the foundation of hive life.[10]

10 Winston, Mark. *The Biology of the Honey Bee.* Harvard University Press. Cambridge, Massachusetts. 1987. 90-101.

SISTERHOOD

In the Hive, we define sisterhood as *a loving, mutually beneficial relationship between two or more women that honors and respects each other's choices—no matter what.*

In today's world, we face immense pressures. We are cooking meals, raising our kids, working, and taking care of our parents… the list goes on. On top of that, we are expected to take care of our health, have a social life, spiritual practice, and workout… It is overwhelming.

It's too much for one woman alone. We are doing too much, often putting ourselves last. This is not sustainable, and worse, it causes disconnection from ourselves and others.

We are designed for *inter*connection. Many of us feel a void without it. We long for women we can travel through life with, those who will be there with us as we age, as our kids grow, as loved ones die, as life happens. We want sisters who will be there with us in our grief, our pain, and our deepest joy, who won't turn away but will just be with us. That is our longing.

Sisterhood. True connection.

But we are walking around with a wound from our past keeping us from that. Healing is required to move forward.

THE SISTER WOUND

The Sister Wound is pain or betrayal inflicted by one woman upon another. Maybe you were deliberately excluded by groups of girls in school, or you've been hurt by gossip. Sometimes, it shows up as competition in the workforce, in parenting, in seeking male attention, and even in family dynamics.

We have both inflicted this hurt and suffered the hurt.

Once we've been wounded, we mistrust other women. The fear of re-experiencing such pain can cause us to guard ourselves against new connections, creating more isolation and loneliness. We may have even convinced ourselves that we are better off alone and can handle life without the support of fellow women.

This builds walls around us, keeping us separate, separate from sisterhood.

Here are some things that keep us from sisterhood. Which do you recognize?

- Fear of being shamed, criticized, unfairly judged, or rejected
- Thinking you aren't as good, successful, or valuable as others
- Judging others as inferior to you, not at your level
- Sensitivity to absorbing other people's energies and emotions
- A mistrust of women, having been the subject of gossip or hurt
- Believing you don't belong or fit in

- A compulsion to control, run things, or fix other people's issues
- Fear of drama or conflict
- Trying to fit in by dimming down or holding back

Everyone has a different experience of sisterhood. Two women approaching the same group might have entirely different experiences based on their past and the wounds they carry.

Until now, perhaps you've never seen examples of healthy relationships between women, or maybe you have. Whether we've learned from our mothers, sisters, aunts, grandmothers, friends, co-workers, or the dramatized betrayals in reality TV, these influences shape our understanding of female relationships.

The bees remind us to move away from conflict, competition, and mistrust and towards support, collaboration, and trust.

In the Hive, sisterhood means we,

- Honor and respect each other's choices, no matter what
- Lift each other up
- Honor our differences
- Speak kindly about one another
- See the best in each other and ourselves
- Love each other through our moments of darkness
- Create spaces to bring all of ourselves and become our best
- Choose to be authentically ourselves

See what shifts in sisterhood when you base it on the Hive Agreements. This is how we heal—one sister at a time.

Bee Fact: Sacred Belonging

From birth, every bee has a place. Even newly emerged workers are instantly welcomed and begin their role without condition. Their scent links them to the colony—to unconditional belonging.[11]

SACRED BELONGING

In Webster's Dictionary, "belonging" is defined as the feeling of being happy or comfortable as part of a particular group and having a good relationship with the other members of the group because they welcome and accept you.

In the Hive, "sacred belonging" is defined as acceptance without conditions from the Divine, yourself, and others.

We all share a deep-seated desire to belong. In our quest for acceptance, we often attempt to conform, molding ourselves into what others expect us to be.

Sacred belonging is anchored in the Divine. It acknowledges that you already belong; there's no need to strive or change to fit in. You don't have to do anything, say anything, or be anything other than yourself to belong. The only requirement is authenticity— simply being you.

---

11 Michael D. Breed. Nestmate recognition in honey bees. Animal Behaviour, Volume 31, Issue 1, 1983, Pages 86-91.

Here are things that may keep you from sacred belonging:

- Feeling misunderstood, unwelcome
- Not knowing where you belong
- Not feeling worthy
- Being intolerant of differences
- Feeling the need to change yourself or tone yourself down to fit in
- Fear of getting hurt
- Not feeling a connection with the Divine
- Feeling the need to be the same

Sacred belonging frees us. You may have felt pressure to change yourself or behave a certain way to fit in, but sacred belonging invites you to show up exactly as you are whether you're sad, happy, worried, lost, or angry. You belong, just as you are. This is the true essence of belonging: acceptance without conditions.

In the Hive, sacred belonging means we,

- Accept all of you
- Ask you to bring your authentic self
- Celebrate our differences
- Know you are inherently sacred and whole
- Don't try to fix, improve, or change one another
- Recognize your Divinely-given gifts
- Know you are part of the sacred makeup of the Hive
- Choose to belong

Having a place of sacred belonging, in turn, allows us to create sustainability.

Bee Fact: Sustainability

Bees only collect nectar when it's abundant and never strip a resource bare. They also pollinate plants as they forage, ensuring that flowers, fruit, and food sources can flourish in return. Bees give back as they receive.[12]

SUSTAINABILITY

In Webster's Dictionary, "Sustainability" is defined as the ability to be maintained at a certain rate or level.

In the Hive, "Sustainability" is defined as choosing actions to live in harmony with ourselves, others, and our world.

In the Hive, we use sustainability as our compass, our north star. When we feel disempowered, lost, out of control, anxious, worried, or disconnected from ourselves or others, we know we are living unsustainably, or out of harmony.

If we are judging ourselves or someone else, we are out of harmony. If we are fighting with a loved one, we are out of harmony. If we are not holding boundaries for ourselves in areas that are important to us, we are out of harmony. If we are struggling financially, we are out of harmony. If we are not keeping agreements with ourselves, we are out of harmony. If we are sick, we are out of harmony.

---

12 Longgood, William. *The Queen Must Die: And other affairs of bees and men.* W. W. Norton & Company, Inc. New York, New York. 1985. 201.

Out of Harmony = Not Sustainable

The areas where we're out of harmony reveal where we're not living sustainably. Once we become aware of this, we can focus our energy on these parts of our lives—bringing ourselves back into balance and choosing more sustainable, authentic ways of living that lead to greater joy and happiness.

Here are some ways you may be living unsustainably:

- Feeling your body is depleted, and you lack energy
- Not having time to do things important to you
- Feeling guilty taking time for yourself
- Not speaking up for what you want
- Giving more than receiving or feeling drained around others
- Not making time for your relationships
- Feeling disconnected from nature or the Divine
- Feeling stuck, frustrated, or resentful
- Feeling like no matter how much you have, it's never enough
- Not knowing what you like, want, or need

When our lives lack sustainability, it affects what we create in our relationships and communities. Reclaiming our life force means recognizing that it is, first and foremost, for ourselves. The decisions about what we give and to whom are choices, not assumptions.

Bees live sustainably. They ensure every member of the hive is supported. If their environment becomes unsuitable, they relocate. Collectively, they produce honey, sustaining their hive (as well as us—thank you, Bees!).

In the Hive, sustainability means we,

- Honor sacred selfishness
- Choose radical honesty
- Trust what is and what is not ours to do
- Trust the choices of our sisters
- Build cooperative relationships
- Do things that are important to us
- Connect with nature and the Divine
- Feel the abundance and support of the Hive
- Choose to live in harmony with ourselves, others, and our world

In the Hive, each woman gets to define what sustainability means to her.

Imagine if we all vowed to live our lives this way. What would be possible? This may feel like a dream, but we don't think so because we are doing it. It takes big dreams to make big changes, and together, we believe we can change the world.

But a mission is only as strong as the foundation it stands on. To live this vision, we follow the Hive Agreements.

PART 4 ~
THE HIVE
AGREEMENTS

The Hive Agreements are six foundational teachings given by the bees to bring harmony to ourselves, our sisters, and the world.

These six agreements align with the hexagon, the interlocking shape that makes up the hive. The hexagon is found in sacred geometry, nature, and ancient teachings on balance, harmony, collaboration, unity, and wholeness.

Imagine sitting in circle with us now… we are about to explore the ancient practices of the hive and the wisdom of the bees.

The Bee Sisterhood invites and inspires women onto the path of harmony through sisterhood, sacred belonging, and sustainability. We align with bee wisdom while following our Hive Agreements:

1. We are Sacred and Whole

We do not see each other as small. We see each other as whole. We hold each other in our highest possibility, even if it doesn't look that way.

2. We All Belong

We accept and love all of you. This is a place where we know each of us already belongs, just as we are. There is nothing we need to do.

3. We Honor Ourselves and Each Other

We believe that all women have a divine guidance system, and we honor how it expresses itself. We do not try to fix each other. We do not gossip. We take up our space.

4. We Learn from Each Other

We get to own, love, and accept all aspects of ourselves in what we see reflected in each of our Hive sisters. We welcome all of each other: the light as well as the shadow.

5. We Live Sustainably

We choose to live in harmony with ourselves, then with others and our world. We no longer create from depletion. We trust ourselves to know what is and is not ours to do.

6. We are Stronger Together

We don't need to do things alone. No bee left behind. We hold your dreams and stories as sacred. We see your desires magnetizing to you right now. We are meant to cross-pollinate.

Come BEE just as you are. Let a Bee be a Bee.

These agreements form the basis of the Hive experiment.

Let's get started…

AGREEMENT #1

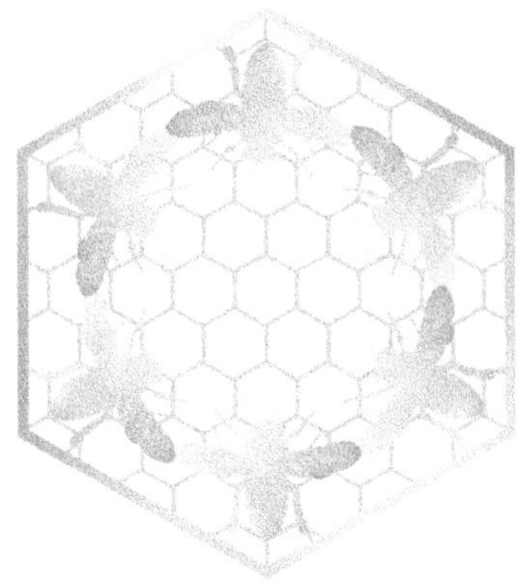

WE ARE
SACRED AND
WHOLE

Agreement #1 ~
We are Sacred and Whole

We do not see each other as small. We see each other as whole. We hold each other in our highest possibility, even if it doesn't look that way.

How would our world be different…

If we accepted ourselves as sacred and whole,
With no need for improvement?

If we knew we had a purpose and place because
We are here, now?

If we saw one another in our greatness,
Celebrating the magnificence and power of
Every single being?

This is the world we are creating.

Bee Fact: We Are Sacred and Whole

Each bee—queen, worker, or drone—has a distinct, purposeful role in the hive. No bee is considered more important than another; their wholeness is defined by their contribution to the greater system.[13]

---

13 Chadwick, Fergus. *The Bee Book: The Wonder of Bees and How to Protect Them for Generations to Come.* Penguin Random House, New York, NY. 2016. 34-36.

We Cultivate Safety

To open ourselves to others, we must first feel safe. If we are worried about backstabbing, gossip, or judgment, we can't trust or be vulnerable with one another.

In our sisterhood, we use our hive agreements to establish safety. These agreements form the foundation that allows us to feel secure, open up, and trust one another.

Maintaining a sense of safety, both within yourself and within the Hive, is crucial.

Part of building safety is acknowledging where we source our security. When we base our security on what others say or think, we will never feel safe. When we choose to base our security on the Divine, our safety and security are sourced from a place that doesn't shift or change.

We are Sacred

Simply being you, being a Bee, you were designed for a purpose. Just like every bee in the hive has a purpose, so do you.

There is nothing you need to prove, no way to improve yourself. There is no effort that needs to happen for you to be of value.

Sometimes, when we get caught up in life, we may forget the sacredness of who we are. We may lose sight of our wholeness.

When you begin to look at yourself and your sisters as sacred and whole, you start to make different choices. You start to look at the bigger picture, connected with the Divine Queen Bee, and remember your place in the Hive.

You stop thinking of yourself as insignificant and realize with the Divine, anything is possible. With the Divine, miracles happen. Relationships can be healed, health can improve, and all your needs, even your deepest desires, will be met.

When the Queen Bee runs the hive, there is more than enough honey for the bees, for the hive, and even enough to share with us so we can put it in our honey cakes and tea.

When you align with your identity as sacred and whole, you see things differently. The things that once troubled you no longer do, and you recognize all the worrying wasn't necessary.

The Divine Queen Bee has got you. You were perfectly designed for the Hive. You are both needed and wanted.

Not only that, you have been designed as an integral part of the Hive with unique, essential gifts. Your path is yours to walk, in your own way, and you get to bring all of you.

WE ARE WHOLE

What would it be like to live in this world where you embrace all of who you are?

You are perfectly created, exactly as you are meant to be. No improvements are necessary. When you release the pressure to constantly improve or conform, you can relax and be with others, free from the need to perform or pretend.

You are unique; there has never been, and will never be, another you.

Wholeness begins with you choosing to believe that all of you is meaningful and welcome in the Hive.

You realize that there is no part of yourself you need to sacrifice or give up. You can bring your whole self into the Hive without cutting off or hiding any parts of who you are. *All* of you is welcome.

Once you recognize your wholeness, you can access your power and sovereignty.

We Claim Our Sovereignty

True sovereignty means recognizing and owning our inherent power and authority over our own lives.

You are the supreme authority in your life.

By collectively embracing our sovereignty, we can shift the dynamics on our planet. When women, in particular, claim their sovereignty, they reclaim their power, their voice, and their right to live authentically and freely.

We choose how we think, feel, express, and connect. When we own our sovereignty, there is a place inside of us that creates peace and power within. It also supports us to trust ourselves and know what is and what is not ours to do.

The Hive honors the sovereignty of every woman standing in her full power, influencing change not through domination but through the undeniable force of self-empowerment and inner strength.

In a beehive, the bees don't ask permission to do their job. They follow their intuition and knowing. This creates divine order.

WE OPEN OUR PERSPECTIVES

When we believe that we are sacred and whole, it helps us see the bigger picture of our lives. We begin to understand our place in it, and how others are part of that picture, too. If I am whole, and I believe you are whole, there is no need to judge or compete. We can honor each other's role.

From this space of wholeness, our energy naturally rises. We automatically raise our vibrational frequency. This shift in perspective is the key to unlocking the miracles, magic, and synchronicity that are always available to us when we align with the Divine, our Queen Bee.

Believing we are whole is a choice.
Our Hive chooses this experiment—to co-create together.

When we deeply know that we are sacred and whole amongst other sovereign and worthy women in a safely held container, what happens next is absolutely breathtaking. A whole new reality opens—one of permission and play, magic, miracles, and synchronicity.

Sacha Buzz

Whether a woman already knows that she is sacred and whole, or she remembers and discovers this truth within the sisterhood, within the Hive, there's an invisible line that is crossed when she knows she is truly safe. All of her emerges.

Very soon after the Bee Sisterhood was formed, my marriage of over a decade came to a close. It was poetic to feel my brokenness and wholeness simultaneously.

During one retreat, Nicole could see my pain and heartache over the end of my marriage. My resolve, fear, and exhaustion were all swirling together; she laid next to me, played one of our favorite songs, curled up beside me, and stroked my hair.

I let go and wept. I felt my pain all the way to the bottom until it alchemized.

Feeling safe to be all of myself—to know I am sacred and whole, and to feel my sisters see and know that, too—gave me permission to bring all of myself. Human and Holy.

When we deeply know that we are sacred and whole amongst other sovereign and worthy women in a safely held container, what happens next is absolutely breathtaking. A whole new reality opens—one of permission and play, magic, miracles, and synchronicity.

I Am Sacred and Whole

Agreement #2

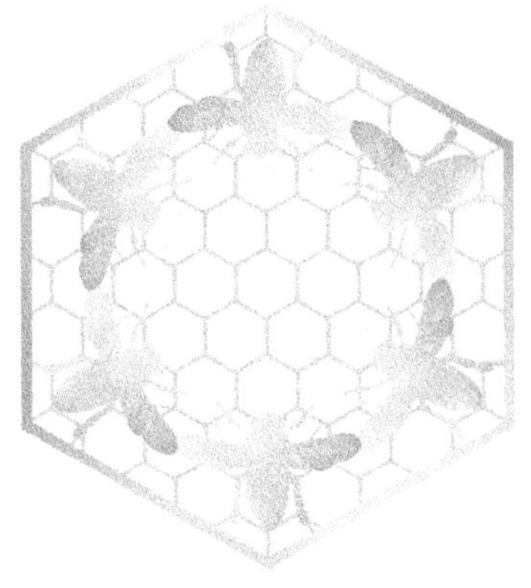

We all Belong

Agreement #2 ~
We all Belong

We accept and love all of you. This is a place where we know each of us already belongs, just as we are. There is nothing we need to do.

The Hive is a place
You already belong
Just as you are.

The Hive is a place
You are loved
Just as you are.

The Hive is a place
You don't need to do anything
But be you.

Breathe that in.

Bee Fact: We All Belong

Bees recognize their own colony members by scent. If a bee carries the right hive pheromone, she is welcomed without question. Belonging is instinctive and non-negotiable in the hive.[14]

---

14 Michael D. Breed. Nestmate recognition in honey bees. Animal Behaviour, Volume 31, Issue 1, 1983, Pages 86-91.

Jennifer Buzz: Where do I belong?

Do I belong? Where do I belong? In the beginning, I had a hard time finding my *value* in all this. I was there when we were gifted the Buzz, but I still didn't feel like I deserved to be in the circle. I had to choose to belong.

It's a continuous choice.

Often, I would choose to step out of sisterhood because I was different. My gifts were different, my vision, or lack thereof, was always different, and it was scary. My sisters were there as sacred witnesses when I was in doubt and suffering. They saw me whole and encouraged me to see a different way of being. In this place, I was able to be present in a new way. Reinvented, I found out that I did not need to have the same talents or vision. In fact, I was special and exceptional because I was different. This is what led me to believe that sisterhood could look different. I now choose to belong.

Being authentic within the Hive has given me freedom.

KNOW YOUR PLACE

"We All Belong" reminds us we have a place. True belonging is about embracing our existence, feeling worthy of being here, and choosing to be fully present in our bodies, our communities, and our world.

When we know we belong, it feels like coming home.

We know who we are and what our purpose is, both within ourselves and in relation to the Hive. When we intentionally shape our self-identity and decide what we want to contribute—and what we don't—we strengthen our sense of power, purpose, and belonging.

Before you can belong to any external hive, you get to find belonging in yourself. Inner belonging is essential for feeling a sense of belonging in other spaces. When we seek belonging and validation outside of ourselves, our sense of belonging will always depend on something or someone external to ourselves.

Belonging is an inside job.

Putting our relationship with the Divine first helps us know who we are. From that place, we can authentically connect with others. It takes a lot of courage to pursue sisterhood and navigate the very normal journey of finding your hive. Knowing we belong because we exist is the first step to being available for belonging to any hive.

You choose the Divine.
You choose you.
You choose us.
And we do, too.

WE LONG TO BELONG

We all long to belong. There's some innate part of us, some drive to be fully seen as ourselves, to not need to do anything to be accepted, honored, and recognized.

Most of us have had experiences of not belonging and the deep pain that it caused. Maybe when you were young, you were laughed at for being different, shunned for your beliefs or for the way you dressed. Or maybe even more recently, when you spoke up, your ideas were not accepted, or your opinion was made wrong.

Not belonging can feel so painful—we will do anything not to feel that pain. We become whoever we need to be and do whatever we need to do to fit in. We start to hide ourselves and not share our authentic thoughts or feelings.

Imagine if the bees didn't feel like they belonged in the hive. What if they looked to one another, asking for permission or validation? How would this affect their hive?

It's the same with us.

By believing we don't belong, we hold ourselves back—our gifts, our talents, our wisdom, our knowing. We try to do it on our own. And when we do that, no one wins.

FEARS OF NOT BELONGING

Some fears and doubts that can hold us back from choosing to belong:

I'm too old.
I'm too young.
I'm too heavy.
I'm too serious.
I'm too busy.
I'm too broke.
I'm too sick.
I'm too poor.

These fears keep us from what we want. They are invisible obstacles in our minds. But what if they weren't true at all? What if these fears were actually keeping us from the Divine, from ourselves, and from the people and resources meant to support our growth and well-being?

Imagine if the bees in a hive started telling themselves they were too old, too young, too busy, or if the Queen Bee or guard bees suddenly decided to take on the roles of the worker bees. The result would be total chaos.

This is a powerful reminder to embrace our true selves and not try to change to fit in. Just like each bee has a unique and vital role within the hive, each of us has our own place and purpose. When we honor who we truly are, without comparison, the hive functions harmoniously and thrives. There's no need to be anything other than who you are; in fact, the health of the hive depends on it.

Belonging is our birthright, a deep knowing that we are already enough just as we are. In this sisterhood, we honor each other's journeys and trust that every one of us is exactly where we need to be, guided by a wisdom greater than our own. This is where true belonging resides—in the acceptance of our own worthiness and the recognition that there is nothing to fix, only love to give.

Belonging is a Choice

Sacred belonging is more than just acceptance—it's the realization that your uniqueness is not only welcomed but essential. Your one-of-a-kind sacred signature—your difference—is what makes you belong. Sacred belonging is about recognizing that you were designed this way—with your thoughts, your gifts, and your quirks—for a specific purpose.

You are a sacred bee.
You belong in the Hive.
There is nothing you need to do except be yourself.

However, being yourself can sometimes be the hardest thing to do. Luckily, being surrounded by others who truly see and appreciate you makes it easier.

Belonging happens when you choose it. The only thing standing in your way is the belief that it doesn't exist or that you aren't meant for it.

Questioning if you belong will cause separation.
Choosing to belong will create connection.

It's like choosing to be married. It's a decision you make again and again. There may be days when you don't feel like you belong, just as there are days you don't feel like being married, but you choose.

There is no magical pill to make you belong, no award to win, no invisible line to cross. You already belong here, just as you are.

As you accept yourself, you accept others. As you accept the parts of you that don't fit in, you recognize they are essential for the health and diversity of the hive.

When born into the hive, the bees don't ask if they belong. They already do, and we believe you do, too.

ACCEPTANCE

Acceptance begins with *you* choosing to believe that you belong in the Hive.

That can be challenging, especially when we have a strong inner critic telling us we're not good enough. When we believe it, it stops us. We need to remember to accept that we belong.

When you accept yourself, you stop judging and naturally begin to accept others. As you come to understand that there's no golden ticket required to enter the Hive and that no one expects you to be anything other than your true self, you start to internalize this truth bit by bit.

This self-acceptance grows and extends to others in the Hive, fostering a community where those unique, "not fitting in" qualities become essential to the Hive's health and diversity.

Not Having It All Together

One main belief that *keeps* women from *choosing* to belong is believing we need to have it *all together* first.

Women hold back from coming out, doing their work, and creating what they want because they think they need to somehow be MORE.

More together.
More experienced.
More happy.
More beautiful.
More organized.
More zen.

That's a lie.
You don't.

You can be depressed,
A "bad" mom,
Unhealthy,
Lonely,
Shy,
A beginner,
Have regrets,
Panic attacks,
A suicidal teenager,
Not know where to start,
Not have experience or a degree,
Be on food stamps,
150 lbs heavier than you want to be,
Going through cancer,
Be divorcing your partner,

Not have "it" all together,
And STILL belong,
Now.

If you're judging yourself as not good enough, ready enough, or healed enough, you're missing the point.

No one **has it together.**
Your humanity is welcome.

This is also an invitation to STOP tearing each other down.
To stop holding each other to a standard of perfection,
Needing each other to be *different*,
Thinking that someone isn't altogether trustworthy means they might be a fraud or a hypocrite.
They're human.
Just like you.
And me.

What if we *embraced* our not-all-togetherness?

Imagine the permission that would give everyone else who is waiting for things to be just right.

Let's turn our woman power ON for each other
Loving each other up,
Cheering each other ON.

What if you don't NEED fixing?

What if you don't need to be
More patient,
More confident,
More creative,
More intuitive,
More together?

What if you don't need to be
Better with money,
Better with your eating habits,
Better with working out,
Better with social media,
Better as a partner, or mom, or friend?

What if you don't need to get rid of your
Anxiety,
Depression,
Worry,
Anger,
Exhaustion?

What if you don't need to stop
Settling,
Filtering,
Censoring,
Controlling,
Regretting?

Most of us have been taught to look at the world through "improvement" glasses.

We are constantly seeing how we need to
Be better,
Do better,
Get rid of things,
Stop doing things…

And if not us, it's our
Kids, partners, friends, family
Or those "other" people who are different from us…
Different religions, parts of the world, races, cultures, and
political parties.

It's a never-ending cycle.
Fixing.
Improving.
Never enough.

But what if we took off those *improvement* glasses?
What if the way you were right *this* second was just right?
What if diversity (different from you) was GOOD?

What if it all belonged just as it is?

I know what you're thinking: *But we want to be better, do better, right?*

There is a difference between
Needing to fix ourselves because we see something *wrong* and
Desiring growth and change because we're *inspired.*

One is from an energy of judgment.
No matter how much you try to change from that place, it will *never* be enough.

The other is from a place of self-love and inspiration,
Not forcing or making ourselves wrong.

Our invitation is to *choose belonging.*

Sister, we want you to know
You don't NEED fixing.
And we hope you take that in,
Because there is a lot of freedom when you know that.

FIT OUT, NOT IN

We all want to belong and feel at home. Maybe you think that means fitting IN. But it doesn't. In fact, it's the opposite.

Fitting IN requires you to change and shift—to hide your most authentic, natural self.

It requires censorship and filtering, avoiding anything that might offend or hurt anyone. It requires constant monitoring to be part of the IN crowd.

Instead, we are inviting you to fit OUT.
Stick OUT, be OUT, as who you really are.

About how you do rituals during the full moon, dance unabashedly when no one is watching, how you hear the voice of your Grandmother when an owl flies past, how you never stick with one thing, how you talk to trees or angels or bees...

Fitting OUT brings attention, and for some of us, we haven't wanted it.

We haven't wanted to be the tall poppy, easily cut down by others.

Better to stay the same height, blend IN, fit IN.
But when you fit IN, your voice sounds like everyone else's.
And then you wonder why you seem invisible, why no one pays attention or listens.

It's not your fault.
Fitting in can help you avoid getting hurt, and no one wants to get hurt.

But here's the truth... we're yearning for OUT.

Coming OUT with your spiritual gifts, your art, your expression, your wisdom, coming OUT with YOU.

OUT brings ease and grace, and a sense of peace because You're no longer tracking what you need to do to fit in. OUT feels good.

Here is your invitation to fit OUT in our Hive.

I Choose to Belong

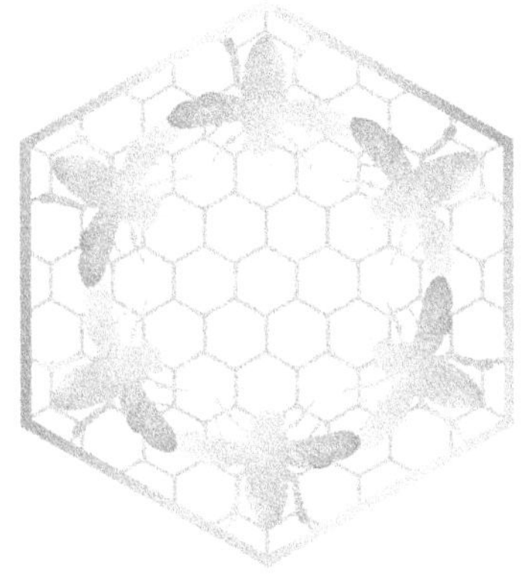

WE HONOR OURSELVES AND EACH OTHER

Agreement #3 ~
We Honor Ourselves
and Each Other

We believe that all women have a divine guidance system, and we honor how it expresses itself. We do not try to fix each other. We do not gossip. We take up our space.

The bees have their own guidance system.
They know how to find flowers to pollinate,
How to make their way back to their hive.

You have your own guidance system, too.
Your own inner wisdom.
In the Hive, we trust that.

We encourage you to listen within,
To trust yourself,
We let go of any need to fix or change one another.

We take up our space
And you take up yours
And there is plenty for all of us.

This is the way we honor ourselves and each other.

Bee Fact: We Honor Ourselves and Each Other

Bees share information through the waggle dance—a non-invasive way to communicate opportunities. Each bee chooses whether to follow the lead based on her own instincts. No bee is corrected or forced.[15]

---

15 Holldobler, Bert & E.O. Wilson. *The Superorganism: The Beauty, Elegance, and Strangeness of Insect Societies.* W.W. Norton & Company. New York, NY. 2009. 175-178.

HOW WE DISHONOR OURSELVES

In Bee Sisterhood, we're changing the world, and yet, there's still a lot of residue from thousands of years of conditioning to examine and release. This shapes the way we do or do not honor ourselves. Some of our behaviors are conscious, but many are not. Let's take a look at a few common ways we dishonor ourselves.

1. Not Speaking Up

Do you ever hold back what you really think? Have you been afraid to speak your truth? Maybe you've stayed silent when you disagreed with your boss or went along with a family vacation you didn't want to take. Perhaps you didn't ask for what you *really* wanted, all in the name of keeping the peace.

But peace isn't the marker of a good relationship. Sometimes, we need truth.

Speaking up as the real, authentic, "too much" parts of ourselves will bump up against others. It might come across the wrong way, accidentally hurting or offending someone. But it also honors you and can create the intimacy you've been craving, awaken a creative channel you didn't know existed, or attract attention to your work and vision.

2. Negative Self-Talk

What thoughts run through your mind? Are they empowering and encouraging, or are they filled with doubt and self-deprecation?

Do you ever tell yourself,
I'm never going to get what I want.

I'm not good enough
No one cares what I think
I can't do that…

These are examples of the critic at work. Focusing on these negative voices attracts more of them. While these thoughts exist, the question is: Which part of yourself do you want to feed? Listening to the empowering, encouraging voice is self-honoring.

3. Staying Small and Not Taking Up Space

Do you feel the need to explain yourself?
Ask for permission to be who you are?

These are signs that you may not be allowing yourself to fully take up your space and shine your fullest. This may look like shrinking or making yourself smaller to make room for others. It may look like staying quiet when you want to speak so you're not an inconvenience or adjusting yourself for others to go with the flow—but at what expense? What if the space needs *you*?

By bringing your whole self, you honor yourself. You deserve to take up all your space.

4. People-Pleasing

We've all wanted people to like us—to appreciate our gifts and hearts. We want to be seen, recognized, appreciated, needed. But trying to make everyone happy is an impossible task. Focusing on the one unhappy person instead of those who already appreciate you leads to self-doubt and questioning your worth.

People-pleasing can lead us to filter what we say, how we create, and what we do. It kills our creativity and intuition, censors our spirit, and makes life less fun. Instead of focusing outward on pleasing others, we focus inward on honoring ourselves and unleashing our truest selves.

5. Over-apologizing

How often do you find yourself saying, "I'm sorry"? As women, we say it all the time. But why? Do we not matter? Do we not deserve to take up space and have our own thoughts and desires? Constantly apologizing sends a message that we don't belong or that what we have to say doesn't matter.

One practice we use in the Hive is shifting from "I'm sorry" to "Thank you." It changes the energy from one of shame to one of gratitude. For example, instead of saying, "I'm sorry I didn't do the dishes," try saying, "Thank you for doing the dishes," or "Thank you for your patience with me." This shift honors you and invites more support and appreciation from others.

6. Not Following Dreams, Desires, Wishes

Your dreams are sacred, implanted within you by the Divine, and ignoring them says that they—and you—aren't important. If you have found yourself not following your dreams, desires, and wishes, you may no longer know what you want.

One of the biggest ways we dishonor ourselves is by denying our own dreams, desires, and wishes. This often goes hand in hand with putting other people's needs first. You might tell yourself that you'll get to your own dreams once you've taken care of everything else, but this delay dishonors not only yourself but also the Divine.

WE DO NOT FIX EACH OTHER

We don't try to fix, improve, or change each other.
This can be hard, especially when it's something we don't like.

We can all fall into the trap of thinking we know better.
But when we try to fix other people's lives for them,
It causes separation.

Nagging, judgment, embarrassment, shame, and guilt don't build relationships.

They tear them apart.

We feel the safest to change when we are loved, respected, seen, heard, and appreciated AS WE ARE.

Every time we get into a major argument, it is because either:
We want the person to be different than who they are, or
They wanted us to be different from who we are.

It hurts when we aren't loved as we are…
That doesn't mean we're perfect.

We all have parts of ourselves we'd like to "improve."
Maybe you would like to be sexually turned on more,
Spend more 1-on-1 time with your family,
Judge everyone, including yourself, less…

There's a big difference between you knowing these parts of yourself and someone else telling you to change or treating you as if you're incompetent.

Words have the power to destroy.
So does trying to manage the lives of others.

As women, many of us have been trained to help others and make them feel better when they are uncomfortable. We give our feedback, ideas, and wisdom away for free; we also give it without permission. We want to help fix the "problem."

Offering unsolicited feedback is criticism.

Instead, to make a relationship work, ask yourself,
Can I love them exactly as they are?
Can I accept them exactly as they are?
Can I trust the Divine is guiding them and doesn't need me to take over for them?

THIS is freedom.
Acknowledging they have a choice.
This is love.
This is our secret.

The most loving thing we can do in sisterhood is honor each other's choices, no matter what. We don't always agree with each other's choices, but we honor them. Choice is freedom, and freedom and sovereignty are our greatest gifts from the Divine.

In the Hive, everyone is equal—no one is considered less or more valuable than another. We don't rank who is *more* important to listen to, who is *less*, who has value, who does not.

WE DO NOT NEED TO BE NEEDED

In choosing to honor each other, we must let go of the *need* to constantly help, support, or fix others.

Caring for others can be exhausting, especially when it feels like an obligation. Some of us don't step into our power and shine brightly because we fear that once we do, *more* people will need us. And we're already tired. So, we unconsciously dim ourselves.

At the same time, a part of us might like being needed. We become indispensable, the go-to person, and it feels good to know we'd be missed if we weren't around. For many women, being needed has become part of our identity—it's who we are. But the reality is that constantly being needed can be draining. Especially when everyone needs you.

What if, rather than being needed, you were valued for who you are and not what you do?

WE DO NOT GOSSIP—THE POWER OF WORDS

One of the most significant factors contributing to mistrust among women is gossip. When we share our sisters' stories and secrets without their permission, we betray their trust. Words have immense power—they can create or destroy. Using words to cut others down, judge, or hurt naturally leads to distance and separation, even if there was no intention to cause harm.

Gossip and talking badly about someone else has become a way to connect with one another. From a young age, many of us are not shown how to truly honor ourselves or each other, leading to comparison and gossip.

But what if we instead used our words to uplift each other? Imagine if our conversations fueled and empowered one another. What if we used our words to paint visions of possibility, to inspire and be inspired by our sisters?

In the Bee Sisterhood, we call ourselves forward to hold each other in the highest light. We choose to speak with intention, using our words to build rather than break. We are here to honor, uplift, and grow together.

BEE COMMUNICATION

In our Hive, there are a few ways we communicate for the health of the Hive. Just as we honor each other and our gifts, it's also important to honor the way each person communicates.

RADICAL HONESTY

Radical Honesty: *Telling the complete, unfiltered truth about your thoughts, feelings, and experiences in the present moment—instead of hiding, sugarcoating, or manipulating information.*

Have you ever found yourself agreeing to something—verbally or nonverbally—that doesn't feel right for you? Have you held back your true thoughts, feelings, or desires? Even though it may feel kind to others, it dishonors you.

In the Hive, we ask for radical honesty—speaking your truth, even if there's a consequence.

Radical honesty starts with telling the truth to yourself, about what you authentically desire, what feels good to you and what doesn't. It creates a resonance of harmony within yourself.

Radical honesty is life-giving and creates deeper relationships built on trust. It's about trusting the guidance system that lives inside each of us.

Nicole Buzz: Radical Honesty

I've been on a deep journey with this idea. From a young age, I stepped into the role of peacemaker—learning to keep the peace and make everyone else happy. That meant doing what I was told, saying the "right" thing, and staying quiet if my words might upset someone. Over time, I became skilled at wearing masks, even saying or doing things that didn't feel authentic to me.

But those masks came with a cost. They created distance between me and my true self, and left me wrestling with an inner conflict: not knowing how to fully share who I am or what I stand for. I also found myself constantly seeking approval and acknowledgment from others, instead of trusting my own inner knowing.

In recent years, I've realized how much this way of being has limited me from truly being seen and connecting with the people in my life. Within the hive, I've been challenged to believe that my message and presence carry a sacred vibration that deserves to be shared, even when it feels unsafe or scary. Radical honesty has asked me to be courageous: to speak my truth, even in the face of fear.

In looking at this journey in my life, I can see how difficult it has been for me to break my patterns of trying to make everyone happy at the expense of myself. For the first time, I feel seen and witnessed by my sisters for who I truly am. I've discovered that even when we disagree, I am still lovable, valuable, and important.

This is a continuous opportunity for me to more deeply connect with myself and although at times, I experience fear around the outcome of what others are going to think or feel about me, the power I am receiving is a deep ability to trust myself—and the Divine—more deeply than I ever imagined. What I couldn't see before is now clear: self-love and a genuine connection with Source can only flow when I stand in my authenticity. This feels like the biggest gift I could ever give myself, and it is what I have always yearned for.

DIRECT COMMUNICATION

Direct communication is vital in our Hive. When we have an issue with someone, we address them directly. We don't talk to anyone else. This prevents misunderstandings and miscommunication. Talking to someone else leads to more conflict and confusion. While this might make you feel better temporarily, it often leads to more conflict and undermines the health of the Hive. When people hear that someone spoke about them to others instead of directly addressing them, it can feel like a betrayal.

By committing to direct communication, we keep our Hive healthy and maintain a loving, kind energy while honoring one another.

PERMISSION TO GIVE FEEDBACK

As part of the Hive, there may be times when you want to share feedback. Perhaps you notice a pattern in a sister that seems destructive, or you see potential in her that you want to call forward. To maintain safety and respect within the Hive, it's essential to always ask for permission before offering feedback.

We trust that every woman has her *own* wisdom and guidance system. She doesn't need your feedback, advice, or wisdom unless she chooses it.

By asking first, we ensure our sister is in the right space, place, and time to receive what you have to offer. You may not know if she simply needs to be witnessed, is in an especially tender place, or is already in clear communication with the Divine Queen Bee. Honoring each other means respecting our choices and not forcing feedback on anyone.

RECEIVING FEEDBACK

On the other hand, there may be times when a sister offers you feedback. It's important to practice honesty in these moments. Just because someone offers feedback doesn't mean you are obligated to accept it. There is no need to be polite at the expense of your own well-being. What matters most is honoring your own needs.

One way to do this is through radical honesty with yourself. Are you open to receiving feedback? If not, what do you need before you can be ready to receive? You might practice radical honesty and say, "No, I am not open to feedback right now."

All of this is important for the health of the Hive. We need honesty about how we are truly feeling and thinking, rather than overriding our own needs to be liked or appear open.

WE HONOR OUR FEELINGS

Many women are experiencing big, conflicting emotions about the state of the world and the overwhelming unsustainability of so many of our systems. It's natural to feel a sense of helplessness and wonder, "Where do we start? Is what we're doing making any difference? Is there any hope? What is truly ours to do in the face of all this?"

In the Hive, we choose to honor these feelings instead of pushing them away. Grief, anger, and despair are all valid responses to the world we live in. They are also fertile ground for revolution and evolution, allowing us to channel our personal and collective sadness and rage into effective action.

Feeling our feelings is not a passive act. It is a radical, revolutionary step essential to building a world of harmony.

SACRED WITNESSING

Every woman needs space to explore her emotions, life path, experiences, and truths, all while being lovingly witnessed by her sisters. The act of sacred witnessing provides the gift of time and presence. For years, the four of us have gathered weekly, beginning with prayer and moving into deep, uninterrupted sharing. We speak until we are completely finished.

In the sacred act of witnessing, we hold space for one another, honor each woman's unique journey, and encourage her to fully embrace the moment and her truth.

Sacred witnessing is one of the most intimate and transformative experiences we can offer one another. It allows us to explore parts of ourselves we might otherwise judge or hide, knowing that in this space, we are accepted as we are. In Bee Sisterhood, we say, "Let a bee be a bee," meaning we don't seek to change one another. Instead, we witness.

As we do, we may say, "I love you no matter what. I trust your process impeccably."

Honoring one another and ourselves invites us into unconditional love for self and our sisters without getting attached to the outcome or timing of their process. This practice not only nurtures deep healing but also strengthens the bonds within our Hive.

Sacha Buzz

One of my favorite parts of the sisterhood is how we communicate with each other. What a gift to know that we all have a divine guidance system and honor how it expresses itself.

When I was preparing to give birth to my rainbow baby, I had a vision for a home birth. I was only met with honor from my sisters.

No fear. No questioning. No projection. No comments of "Are you sure that's safe as an almost 40-year-old mom? Don't you think you need a backup plan?"

The gift of taking up my space and being honored in my truth by my sisters led to me experiencing my dream home birth in my bathtub with my new husband by my side and my teenage daughters there to witness me in my power.

WE HONOR OUR BOUNDARIES

Each woman in the Hive sets her own boundaries, and we honor them.

For instance, if a sister prefers not to receive unsolicited advice, she can say,

- Thank you, but I'm not interested in advice at this time,
- No, I am not available to sacred witness right now. Can you ask another Bee Sister?
- I'd like to be witnessed without advice. I'm focusing on listening to myself at this time.

In Bee Sisterhood, we invite you to set the boundaries *you* need to feel respected and supported.

We honor each individual sister.
We honor her choices.
We honor and celebrate her boundaries.

This maintains a healthy and thriving Hive.

I HONOR MYSELF AND MY SISTERS

AGREEMENT #4

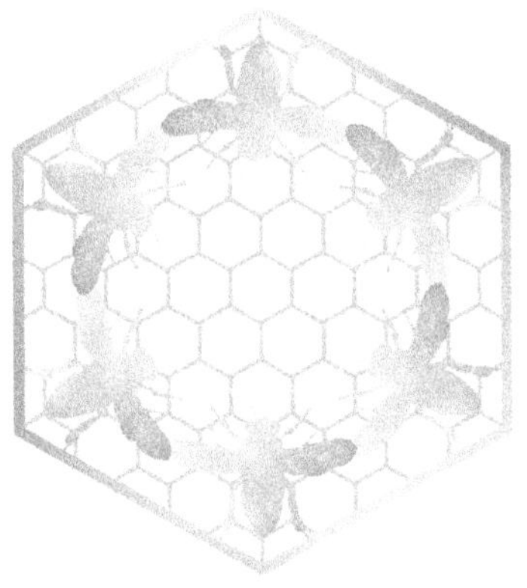

WE LEARN FROM EACH OTHER

AGREEMENT #4 ~ WE LEARN FROM EACH OTHER

We get to own, love, and accept all aspects of ourselves in what we see reflected in each of our Hive sisters. We welcome all of each other: the light as well as the shadow. No bee left behind.

What if every person you met was your teacher?
If every encounter, a sacred moment
To grow, learn, and love?

What if you welcomed all of your sisters?
The beautiful, kind, loving parts and
The ugly, mean, shameful parts?

What if instead of wanting everyone to be like us,
We welcomed diversity
And knew it was vital to the health of the Hive?

Bee Fact: We Learn from Each Other

Bees use social learning to find food and navigate. They observe other bees' dances and choose to explore based on trust. Watching one another enhances individual growth.[16]

---

16 Johnson, Brian. (2010). Division of labor in honey bees: form, function, and proximate mechanisms. Behavioral ecology and sociobiology. 64. 305-316.

A Spiritual Approach to Relationships

Here in Bee Sisterhood, we take a spiritual approach to relationships, which means we embrace them as part of our growth, learning, and deeper purpose.

We aren't created to do things alone.

We are designed to be interdependent, and the bees perfectly model how to be in life-giving relationships based on mutual support, not codependency.

Choosing to be in relationships with the intention of spiritual growth opens up infinite possibilities. From this stance, our relationships become opportunities for healing, innovation, and the co-creation of the harmonious world we desire.

Light and Shadow

In our Hive, we know there is magic in both our light and dark. We welcome *all* parts of one another, especially the parts we have hidden away.

What would our world look like if we no longer felt the need to hide parts of ourselves, if we felt safe to be real and open about it all? If we accepted or even embraced the light and the dark within ourselves? If we knew our sisters also embraced us without judgment?

It takes courage to lean into the parts of us we have hidden away. By acknowledging and accepting these hidden parts, confronting fears, insecurities, and past traumas, we can consciously bring all of ourselves to the Hive. This brings more balance and authenticity. It also transforms our perceived weaknesses into strengths, cultivating a more integrated sense of self.

When we don't embrace ALL of who we are, when we don't acknowledge our darker aspects, they can come up unexpectedly, sometimes explosively, hurting ourselves and those around us. This can damage the Hive. So, we choose to bring our hidden parts forward. We accept and embrace them within ourselves and one another.

Growth happens in safe relationships.

WE ARE MIRRORS FOR EACH OTHER

We all have parts of ourselves we can't see—parts that unknowingly hold us back from what we truly want. Sometimes we know what's sabotaging us, and sometimes we don't. This is where our Hive comes in.

Our sisters help us see what we can't on our own.

Do you find your sister bossy? There is somewhere you are, too. Do you think your mother-in-law is critical? Yep, you are, too. Find your partner controlling? Where are you controlling? Don't like uncommitted people? There is somewhere you are uncommitted…

All those things that annoy and bother you about someone else are actually reflections of yourself. It is the same with our brilliance.

Love her confidence? There is a place where you are highly confident. Admire your friend with an adventurous spirit? That spirit lives within you, too. See the compassion in your co-worker? You are compassionate, too. Have the most loyal sister ever? You are loyal, too.

In the Hive, we acknowledge that *everything* we see in our sisters is a mirror of ourselves. What we see and say about another sister is also something we must own within ourselves, whether it is positive or negative.

What we believe about others reflects what's within us. These reflections—both the ones we resist and the ones we admire—are teachers, teaching us about ourselves, the parts and areas we can't see on our own.

WE INVITE BEES BACK IN

When a sister disappears from the Hive, we reach out and invite her back in. There are times when we feel inadequate or separate, and when you're alone in those feelings, it can be hard to see yourself as whole. Breakdowns happen, but they can also be doorways to the breakthroughs you need to move forward in your life. Doing this on your own isn't always possible, or it might take much longer than necessary.

The Hive calls you forward into the reality of what is. We witness you in your shame or grief and help you remember that you are more than those parts—more than the doubt, criticism, or separation that are running in the background. The Hive won't let you stay stuck in your pain. Instead, it invites you to realign with the truth.

As a Hive, we choose to stand for each other. If we notice a sister missing or quieter than usual, we check in—not out of co-dependence or a need to fix, but out of genuine care. We feel your absence, and we want you to know you're missed, and we're here for you.

Nicole Buzz: Mirroring

Over the past 4 years, one of the most profound gifts I have received from my sisters is the gift of mirroring. Earlier, I shared my own personal story of how I would compare myself with other women and how it was causing me pain and separation. I believe this happens regularly between women and is often taught early in life.

Through my journey of sisterhood, I saw that this pattern didn't serve me in any way, nor did it bring me joy or happiness. It was time for me to show up differently and break this habit.

I am very committed to my life and my transformational work, which is calling me forward. One of the practices I have been taught is Mirroring—the idea that we are all mirrors for one another. We are all here to show each other areas that we may not see for ourselves—our blind spots.

In this practice, I choose to really allow my sisters to be my mirror. When I notice my sister doing something amazing or something that I really admire, I own that those traits also live inside me. I take the opportunity to say to myself, "She is amazing, and so am I." If I see her as powerful and strong, then I also get to see myself as powerful and strong. I can build her up and witness her in all of her amazing gifts and rise alongside her. I believe this is what is meant by "Rise, sister, rise."

I can also look at the shadow, or negative, as well. If I notice a sister is being judgmental or hurtful to someone, instead of criticizing her and saying something negative about her, I can use this as an opportunity to look within myself. We all have it all. She is giving me a gift to recognize those same traits live within me. She shines light on it and brings attention to it. If I say that woman is so judgmental inside my mind, then I get to ask myself, "Where am I judgmental?" If I think a woman is being disrespectful to her husband, where am I being disrespectful to my husband? The places this practice allows me to go within myself are beyond anywhere I could go alone. I learn from my sisters, and because of this, it has been one of my greatest gifts.

Bee Fact: We Honor Diversity

Genetic diversity within a hive, resulting from the queen mating with multiple drones, creates bees with different temperaments, learning styles, foraging preferences, and immune strengths. This diversity makes the hive more adaptable, resilient, and successful in changing conditions.[17]

17 Mattila HR, Seeley TD. Genetic diversity in honey bee colonies enhances productivity and fitness. Science. 2007 Jul 20; 317 (5836): 362-4.

WE LEARN FROM DIVERSITY

When everything is the same, life can become boring. Imagine eating the same meal for dinner every night; eventually, you would crave variety. Not only would it become dull, but your body would also miss out on the array of nutrients it needs.

The same thing applies to the people we surround ourselves with. Spending time only with those who share the same beliefs, ideas, and backgrounds can limit our growth and understanding.

If you look at an ecosystem, homeostasis is not healthy. The more diverse an ecosystem is, the healthier it is. It is the same in our Hive—the diversity of the hive strengthens it.

We welcome people who think differently, who challenge our beliefs, and who choose to walk different paths.

Differences create diversity. So, in the Hive, we welcome differing opinions. We invite people to speak up, even if it's not what everybody else thinks. The Hive welcomes it all.

Amber Buzz: Different is Good

One of my good friends is Ann. We are not alike, and I like that.

We met in college. I don't know exactly how we became friends… I'm woo-woo. She is conservative. I own an online business. She is retired. I'm married with kids. She's never been married, no kids. I wear flashy clothes. She likes cargos with collared shirts. Our politics are opposite. And yet…

We both knit, play the ukulele, love our families, to travel, grow and learn. I learn a lot from my friend Ann.

It is seductive to only want to be with people we are like, no one to challenge our thinking or beliefs.

What if instead, you invited diversity?

No matter their "frequency," their religion, their politics.

Having sisters who are different from us keeps us from categorizing people into "Us vs. Them," reminding us that we are part of one human family, no matter how we vote, pray, spend, or dress.

We don't have to like the same things to like each other.

Being with the same people, thinking the same, doing the same, keeps us the same. And maybe you want that… like you want to hang out with other creatives to KEEP you creating or spiritual people to KEEP you connected to God.

But if you want to change, to be inspired, motivated, and awakened, it's time to do something different.

When I want to be inspired, I don't go and listen to people who think the same way I do. When I want to create something I haven't before, I don't do the same things I've done before.

If you want change, you need to do something different, meet someone different, embrace the different.

WE CELEBRATE EACH OTHER

In the Hive, there is no pyramid of power. We no longer need to compete and rise above one another to succeed. Instead of comparing ourselves to other women, judging, critiquing, or even praising them, we choose to not place ourselves in an imaginary hierarchy. We choose celebration and collaboration.

In ancient times, women would gather to celebrate each individual's unique gifts—a sacred practice that has been largely lost in modern cultures. Bee Sisterhood is reviving this tradition of mutual celebration, thereby bringing our sisters into a harmonious frequency—the frequency of the bees.

What if, by celebrating another person, nothing was taken away? What if celebration actually magnetized more to you, as well? What if everyone could grow in love, abundance, and compassion? What if there weren't winners and losers?

When we celebrate another woman, we turn our attention towards it. We call it in. We magnetize it. We become it. It inspires us and calls us forward, as well.

You are that.
All of it.

Jennifer Buzz:
I Love That About You

The act of celebrating our fellow sisters, even those we don't personally know, helps us celebrate ourselves as well. I once found myself judging women who dressed differently than I did, only to realize that such judgments were ultimately a reflection of my insecurities. By shifting my perspective and admiring how a woman could confidently wear an outfit, saying, "Wow, she is really rocking that outfit," I was not only celebrating her but also embracing and celebrating myself and every woman.

In the Hive, when a sister shares a shadowy or shameful part of herself, we often respond with, "I love that about you." This opens the door for acceptance and healing, reinforcing that she is sacred and whole, just as she is. This creates a sustainable energy within by boosting our self-love. We then naturally feel more deserving of belonging. This can eliminate doubt, allowing us to fully believe we are worthy of being part of the Hive.

I have done a ton of work on myself in this area, and it has been one of the most powerful things I have done. I've made a conscious choice to celebrate all aspects of my sisters. I own their gifts as my gifts and recognize their obstacles as mine. Women are my greatest teachers and a bridge into myself.

I LEARN FROM MY BEE SISTERS

AGREEMENT #5

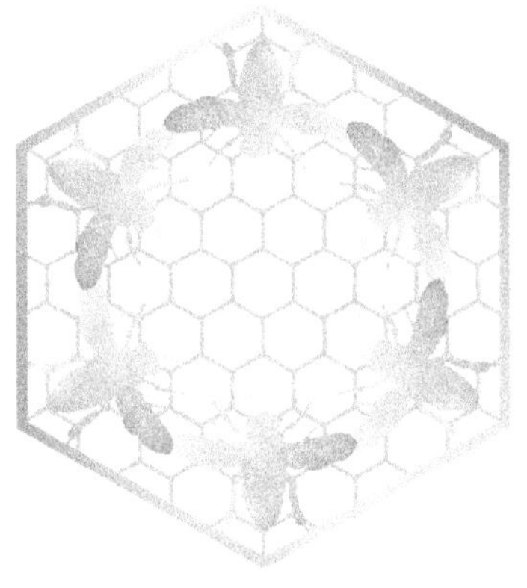

WE LIVE SUSTAINABLY

Agreement #5 ~ We Live Sustainably

We choose to live in harmony with ourselves, then others and our world. We no longer create from depletion. We trust ourselves to know what is and is not ours to do.

Imagine what it would feel like to live in harmony
With ourselves, our sisters, our world,
If we no longer gave to the point of depletion,
If we took care of our bodies, our spirits, our dreams,
If we found a way to be in relationships that felt nourishing?

Imagine no longer feeling the need to make sure everyone else is doing what they need to do, letting go of the worry that comes from trying to take care of it all, and having the space and time to do what you're meant to do.

The way we create harmony within our hive begins with personal accountability for the sustainable or unsustainable choices we make daily and actions we take—how we show up, how we treat ourselves and others, how we use our energy and resources, and how we interact with the world. It begins with us—one bee at a time.

Bee Fact: We Live Sustainably

Bees instinctively avoid overworked flowers and shift to more abundant nectar sources. They forage in balance, never depleting the same resource repeatedly.[18]

18 Longgood, William. *The Queen Must Die: And other affairs of bees and men.* W. W. Norton & Company, Inc. New York, New York. 1985. 201.

DEPLETION VS. SUSTAINABILITY

As women, most of us have been taught to take care of, help, and support others before our own needs and desires. Unfortunately, it has a cost—depletion. Depletion of our health, ideas, vitality, energy, and creativity.

It's easy to fall into depletion, where you constantly give more than you have, leaving yourself drained. This can happen in many areas of life—maybe with your teenager, a work project, your partner, or even a creative project that leaves you feeling exhausted. You get stuck thinking you have to do it right, do it better, or make others happy. So you give, and give, and give yourself away.

Instead, we get to learn sustainability.
We get to learn what sustains us instead of depletes us.

Here's a list of activities that often deplete our energy:

- Over-giving and over-worrying about our kids, partners, or parents
- Cooking dinner after a long day at work
- Doing work for free
- Jumping on calls to give free advice
- Over-caring about what others think
- Taking others' opinions over your own
- Lacking in self-care practices

If something depletes your energy, consider how to remove it or find a way to make it feel more sustainable.

SACRED SELFISHNESS

Many of us have been taught as women not to be selfish. It is especially prominent for women. We're told by our mothers and grandmothers that, as women, one of the best things we can do is to take care of others. To be other-centered. Women are often the primary caregivers, looking after children, the elderly, and their communities, filling in the gaps wherever they are needed.

We've also been warned against being "selfish," and many women don't learn to focus on their own needs until later in life, if ever. For some, this realization comes during menopause, a time when children may have left home, careers have been established for decades, and long-term relationships have settled into routine. It's then that many women look back and realize they've spent much of their lives giving themselves away to others.

Often, women recognize that they've postponed their own dreams and desires, telling themselves they would pursue them after fulfilling certain responsibilities. But as those milestones pass, they find new obligations to occupy their time, energy, and creativity. Aging brings a shift for many women, a sense of freedom as they begin to care less about the expectations and obligations imposed by others. This makes it easier to choose sacred selfishness, as women know themselves, love themselves, and choose when and how to share their gifts with others.

Sacred selfishness is essential to the hive. It is self-honoring. We focus on ourselves and what sustains us first. A bee can't support the hive if it is depleted or dead. We don't sacrifice ourselves for the Hive. We find a sustainable path that allows us to serve the Hive long-term. The health of the hive is directly reflected in the health of its bees.

When we prioritize our own needs and fill ourselves first, we shift from merely doing service to truly being in service and are sourced to do so.

Amber Buzz: Potency in the Pause

I know what it's like to automatically say Yes, ignoring the part of me that needs to rest, to listen within and slow down.

I'm a mom of two now grown men, a wife, and a business owner. I've got friends, family, clients and a team who rely on me and there is a still a part of me who feels a need to not let anyone down, to make people happy. But by doing that, I've also overridden my need to rest.

When I first started my company, I didn't think I had time to pause. After years of hustling and taking care of everyone else, I hit my wall. I ended up in the hospital with pneumonia and almost died.

As I laid in that hospital bed, with my son crying in my arms, I realized I couldn't do it anymore. My own mom died when I was thirteen and I wouldn't do that to my boys. Things had to change.

I considered shutting my company down for good, but that felt wrong. My work is my mission. I just needed to figure out a different way to do it.

So, I took a pause.

I went on retreat for three weeks.
I didn't plan a thing.
I laid in a hammock.
I journaled.
I took naps.
I reflected.

I consciously chose to stop producing, stop giving, stop creating. Pausing brought me back to what felt sustainable for me.

It has now been over a decade since my time in the hospital. I've made pausing my way of life. I take a weeklong pause every month to rest. The longer I lead, the more I recognize that the pause is vital for the longevity of my giving. Not only that, I have found I am way more productive and creative with rest.

Just like the bees who, in the winter, bring their buzz to a very soft hum as they rest, there is also a time for us to rest.

LETTING GO OF CONTROL

Part of being in the Hive is learning to let go of control. When you're making decisions for yourself, you may feel you have control, but when you join a group, that's no longer the case—you have to trust.

Trust is earned. It's also a choice.

Perhaps your first step in trust is joining the Hive, thinking, *Let's see if this works.* Over time, as you connect with others, share your gifts, and witness others standing by you, even when things get tough, you begin to build trust in these relationships. Eventually, you realize those around you truly have your best interests at heart.

For the OG Bees, we each have had to let go of control. With four of us running the company, there are times when one of us has a strong idea, and another might disagree. But when we trust the other person has our best interest at heart, we can let go of the need to have things our way.

At first, letting go of control can be scary, but the more we let go, the more space, time, and energy we gain. For example, if we're controlling everything—bringing in the money, managing the spending, planning the menu, paying the bills, taking care of the plants, organizing the kids' schedule—that's a lot of work. But when we let go of control and surrender to the natural rhythm of the Hive, we find freedom and ease.

Being part of the Hive means you don't need to be in control all the time. Letting others do their jobs leads to greater freedom for you and them. This supports us to create a sustainable life.

Control can also show up in more subtle ways, like keeping ourselves isolated or not using our voices—this, too, is a form of control that doesn't serve us or the Hive.

Control often stems from a lack of trust in the Divine Queen Bee. We feel it's our job to run the show. When we try to control everything, we miss out on collaboration, and the outcome is limited to one person's perspective.

Part of stepping into the Hive is learning to trust.
What would you do if you radically trusted the Divine?
What would you do if you radically trusted yourself?
What would you do if you radically trusted your Sisters?

What would that change?
Trust *supports a sustainable life.*

WE CHOOSE FAITH

When we *don't* trust the Divine Queen Bee, we try to control our world and the worlds of others in order to feel safe and secure. We get worried that we won't be taken care of. This is the same belief that breeds competition and fosters the illusion of scarcity.

At the deepest root, it is not trusting in the benevolence of the universe.

Faith relaxes you. It diminishes your worries and gives you a greater sense of peace. When you feel peace, you are able to see more opportunities and possibilities. You also are willing to try things you haven't tried before. You aren't afraid to fail because you know no matter what happens, the Divine has you and knows what she's doing. You are part of the sacred makeup of the Hive.

What doorways open when you live with faith?

LET A BEE BE A BEE

How many times have you thought, "This person would be better off if they just did this one thing?" If they were quieter, more successful, better with their children, or took better care of themselves. We do this with our spouses, children, friends—everyone.

These thoughts are judgments. And when we judge others, we're also judging ourselves. The level of judgment we place on others often mirrors how harshly we judge ourselves.

Judgment often leads to a desire to fix things, right? If we think we know how someone should be, we naturally assume we know how to fix them. How often do you tell someone in your life what they need to do? We're perpetuating a broken system.

What if, instead, we believed every person has their own internal guidance system with all the answers they need? What if we empowered them to trust themselves and listen to that inner voice guiding them?

Sometimes, we feel like we know better, but what if their guidance is meant to lead them in a different direction? By stepping in, we might cause harm or make them doubt themselves. What if trying to "fix" others only creates frustration for us and doesn't help them?

This brings us to what we call in the Hive, "Let a bee be a bee." When we try to change someone, our energy goes out to them, distracting us from our own path and purpose.

Think about it: We have limited mental and emotional space. When we fill that space with worry and concern for others, we crowd out our thoughts, dreams, and feelings. Focusing on someone else's journey disempowers them and neglects our own growth. We create a burden on ourselves that we can't lift because it's not ours to carry.

This way of living leaves us feeling overwhelmed, exhausted, fearful, and disconnected from others and ourselves.

The Bee sisterhood invites you to let this go. We invite you to return to let a bee be a bee and trust others to follow their bee guidance. When you do this, you'll be amazed at the freedom it creates. This might be a big challenge for some of us, but it's also an incredible opportunity for more freedom than you could ever imagine.

When we focus on our own bee guidance, we create sustainability.

WHAT IS YOUR LEVEL OF SUSTAINABILITY?

Let's take a look and see where you may or may not be sustainable. Within Bee Sisterhood we assess ourselves and our lives using the following eight categories.

Spirituality

How is your relationship with the Divine? Do you feel a connection with something bigger than you? What is your relationship to receiving and faith?

Self

How is your connection with yourself? How do you treat yourself? Do you value yourself? Do you focus on your needs and desires?

Body

What is the condition of your health? Are you taking care of your body, or do you prioritize everything else? Are you in partnership with your body, or do you treat it like a machine?

Family

What is your relationship like with your family? Do you respect one another or hide things from one another? Do you feel love and acceptance?

Partnership

Are you in a loving partnership with someone? If not, are you satisfied with the way things are? Or do you feel a sense of lack?

Community/Sisterhood

Do you have a community? Do you have sisters you can connect with who support you in good times and bad?

Purpose/Work

Do you have a sense of purpose? Do you feel fulfilled and satisfied with the energy you're putting in and what you're receiving in return?

Finances

How do you feel about your finances? Are your needs well met? Do you experience a sense of abundance or scarcity when it comes to money?

HIVE SUSTAINABILITY WHEEL

When you look at the full wheel, you might see areas that feel out of balance or calling for more attention.

Maybe your finances are going well, but your health isn't. Or maybe you're really connected in your relationships, but you don't feel on purpose.

Sacrificing one piece for the other isn't sustainable. Living sustainably means you are in harmony with yourself, others, and the world.

To take the full assessment, turn to the back of the book or head over to **www.beesisterhood.com/quiz** to take the quiz and see what area you're called to bring into harmony at this time.

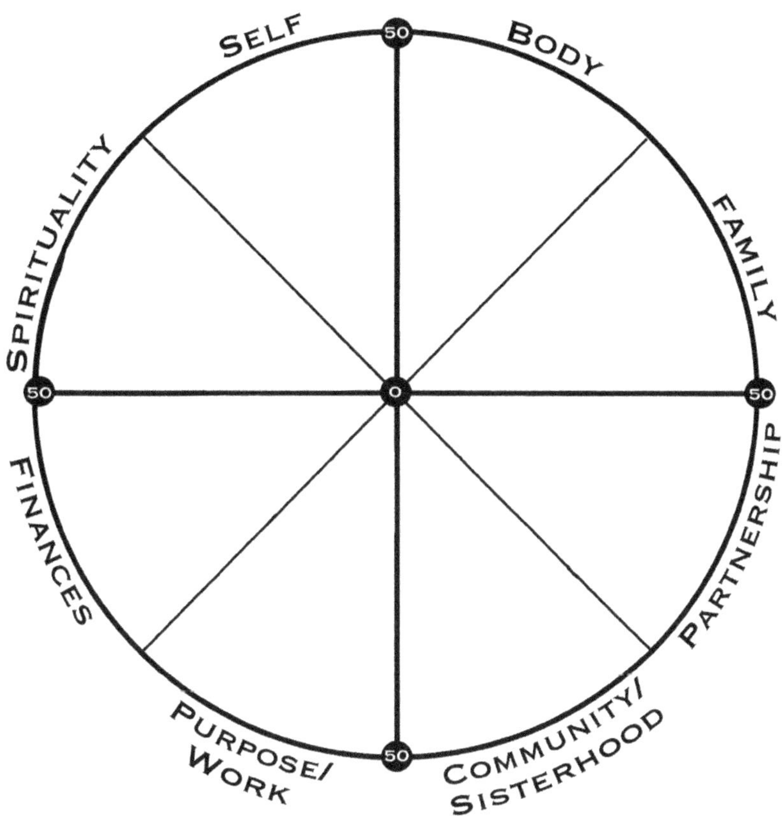

SELF
50
BODY
SPIRITUALITY
FAMILY
50
0
50
PARTNERSHIP
FINANCES
PURPOSE/
WORK
50
COMMUNITY/
SISTERHOOD

BUILDING A SUSTAINABLE WORLD

By one woman creating a sustainable life, we begin to create a sustainable world. But how does that actually work? When we aren't living sustainably, when we are taking care of other people to our own detriment, there isn't enough for us to give to anyone else. We are in a perpetual state of survival.

We are choosing more than just survival here. We're building a different world.

We begin by connecting with the Divine Queen Bee, trusting and having faith that we are sacred and whole. We choose sacred belonging, trusting that we are here for a purpose and trusting in the Divine unfolding.

Next, we connect with ourselves, creating sustainability in our own world. We do not allow ourselves to be depleted or overwork ourselves to the point of burnout. We become someone who is able to give and receive.

Once we do that, our sustainability moves into our community. Our sisters and friends start to see the difference in us. Maybe our health shifts, we are more patient with our kids, or we're less anxious. Our friends and sisters ask, "What is your secret?" At that time, you can share the Bee Sisterhood and Hive Agreements. You may even pass along this book (*wink wink*).

Maybe you start to build sustainable relationships that feed you. Maybe you partner with your neighbor and share vegetables, or share childcare with a fellow mom. As you start going on walks with your neighbor, you both get healthy. As you lean into your own personal sustainability, it starts to affect the ecosystem of your family, your friends, and your community.

And sister by sister, community by community, the Hive starts to take over the world. Sustainability becomes more than just simply taking care of your own needs. It supports the world. This is what we are doing at Bee Sisterhood.

Your decision to live sustainably becomes the action that changes our world.

I Choose to Live Sustainably

Agreement #6

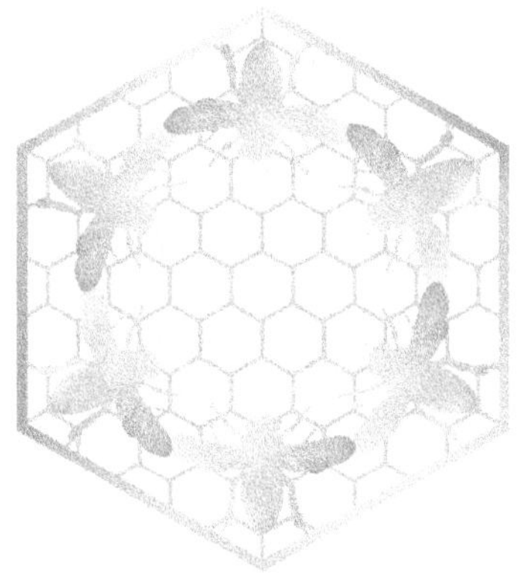

We are Stronger Together

AGREEMENT #6 ~ WE ARE STRONGER TOGETHER

We don't need to do things alone. We hold your dreams and stories as sacred. We see your desires magnetizing to you right now. We are meant to cross-pollinate.

What if all you needed was available?
All the resources, ideas, and inspiration?
The guidance, help, and support?
Love, compassion, and healing?
What if you had it all?

You do.
But not alone.
We are meant to be together.

Bee Fact: We are Stronger Together

Bees rely on each other to survive. They regulate temperature together, share food, groom one another, and collectively defend the hive. One bee alone cannot survive.[19]

---

19 Seeley, Thomas D. *Honeybee Democracy.* Princeton University Press. Princeton, New Jersey. 2010. 9, 29.

Alone vs. Together

When a bee leaves the hive, it doesn't survive for long. Bees are meant to thrive *within* the hive. Everything they need for sustenance comes from it. Without it, they die. The same is true for us as women. We often try to do everything on our own, but we weren't designed for isolation. We were designed for interconnection.

Maybe in the past, you've tried being in a group, and it didn't work. But there is only so much you can do alone.

Imagine a single bee trying to do everything needed for the hive— laying eggs, exploring the area, defending the hive, pollinating, and caring for the young. One bee could never manage all of these tasks alone. Yet, as women, we often try to raise families, nurture relationships, succeed in our careers, maintain our health, be happy, make a difference in our communities, and stay spiritually connected—all alone.

We are not meant to be on our own.
We are meant to be together.
All of the Hive is needed.
You are needed.

Research shows that when we work together, we're
More likely to complete our goals,
Have a lot more fun.
Come up with better ideas,
Are less distracted,
More accountable…
Even our IQ increases.

Everything changes when we work together.

HIVE JOBS

In the hive, each bee has a purpose.

The queen bee is necessary for the health and survival of the hive. She lays eggs.

There are drone bees whose job is to fertilize the queen bee. There are some bees whose job is to scout locations for new hives. Sister bees go out and collect pollen. Nurse bees take care of young pips or baby bees. Guard bees help protect the entrance of the hive.

Each bee has a purpose and a different job. Each one doing their job is what makes the hive stronger.

Can you imagine if there were no guard bees? No one to check to see if any disease-infected bees came in? Or no bees to check that someone came in from another hive and took all the resources? The hive is stronger together.

We are stronger together.

We are here to cross-pollinate. To share resources, knowledge, and wisdom. The more we cross-pollinate, the easier things get.

WE SEE YOUR GIFTS

Just as we need others to help us see how we might be harming ourselves or dimming our light to fit in, the same is true when it comes to recognizing our gifts. It can be challenging to truly see our own brilliance because what we've done naturally our whole lives often just feels normal to us. But to someone else, those things might be needed, wanted, and even magical.

One of the benefits of being in the Hive is the reflection from others who can see your gifts and tell you about them. Perhaps you've always had a way with animals, intuitively sensing when someone's heart is aching without them saying a word, listening deeply without trying to fix someone in their pain, seeing visions of the future, effortlessly making money, or inspiring others just by being present. Every one of these gifts is vital in the Hive.

Every. Single. One.

SHARING GIFTS

After first connecting with the Divine Queen Bee and then tending to yourself—taking a personal inventory of sustainability and self-care—it's time to shift your focus outward toward the Hive.

Being Hive-focused means bringing your unique gifts to the collective. That starts with recognizing you have them. Wherever you are in your journey, you have wisdom, experiences, learnings, and gifts to offer the hive.

The Hive isn't just a place where we bring our gifts, uncover hidden parts of ourselves, or discover more about who we are— it's so much more than that. A hive is meant to function in deep interconnection, like one big, living organism. If one part of the hive is struggling, another part steps in to support it.

One sister might need another's gift. There are things she may not be good at or simply doesn't want to do, and that's when she can speak up and ask others to share their gifts. Chances are, someone else in the Hive is an expert and loves doing it.

Have you ever had a burning question answered through the words of another, exactly what you needed to hear at just the right moment? This is what we do for each other in the Hive. We share our thoughts, expressions, and worries with the Hive, and often, the inspiration or solution we need comes from another sister.

When women are invited into leadership, there's a tendency to hesitate, to hold back, feeling it's just another responsibility added to an already full plate. But this isn't about taking on more. It's about stepping into leadership by using your most natural gifts—the ones that feed your soul. When you offer these gifts, you're not only serving yourself, but you're also supporting others in the process.

To share your gifts, you need to believe you have them, trust that giving won't deplete you, and know that there is purpose in sharing them. We all want our contributions to be witnessed and valued. And by bringing your authentic gifts to the Hive, you nourish both yourself and the collective.

What if your gift is exactly what is needed?
What if there was a sister waiting for your unique gift?
What if holding your gifts back hurt the Hive?

This is a call for you to share your gifts with the Hive. As each of us steps into our gifts, the entire Hive elevates together. Bring your gifts. They are vital to the Hive.

Jennifer Buzz: My Truest Gifts

As part of this Hive, I have found that my gifts are different from those around me. My gifts do not really fit into a list. They tend to be more energetic and less tangible. By choosing to be in a group of women who fully choose to see me for my whole self, I have been able to own my truest gifts with celebration.

Your gifts may not be obvious, but the hive NEEDS your gifts. You may not even see your gifts as special. We are suggesting that you are special and sacred even when your gifts don't look like everyone else's.

CROSS-POLLINATION

When bees are out gathering pollen, they'll transfer it from one flower to another, from plant to plant. This is called *cross-pollination*. By doing so, fertilization happens, and this genetic mixing leads to healthier crops and ecosystems.

It's the same in the Hive. We transfer our ideas, beliefs, visions, resources, wisdom, learnings, expertise, and solutions to one another.

When we are together in a Hive, we start to cross-pollinate. We recognize that anything is possible. We start to see more possibilities inspired by others in the hive. We begin to really know ourselves and learn our individual gifts. The Hive brings those possibilities to us.

When others see our gifts and hold our vision, we start to believe in ourselves and our capabilities even more. There are things that are available all around you that you cannot see. There are things your mind cannot conceive of. There are experiences that others have had that you could never believe existed. This is the power of the Hive. We open doorways for one another.

One way we cross-pollinate in the Hive is by finding sustainable solutions. We don't just look for solutions or things that will work for one group or that are good for one part of the Hive. We look for solutions that are good for everyone.

We cross-pollinate not only solutions but visions of our Hive. Part of the vision we've created through cross-pollination is one that creates sustainability for you, your family, your community, and the world.

Cross-pollination makes us stronger.

A Faster Path

Most of us believe we should be able to figure "it" out on our own. Maybe you've spent six months going back and forth about which business to start, only to hire a business coach and make a decision in less than a week. Maybe your baby has had colic and been crying for months, but with one conversation with another mom, you're no longer eating garlic, and the baby is sleeping through the night. Maybe you envisioned holding a women's circle but couldn't decide on a location for months, until one conversation with a friend instantly gave you the dates and location.

It's hard to see our own resistance when we're caught in it. There are always distractions keeping us from what we need to do, pulling our focus elsewhere. But here's the truth: Getting support does not make us weak.

Support = Speed

Sure, you can go it alone and take the long way, but the Divine Queen Bee has placed someone in the Hive who holds the map to get you exactly where you want to go—faster. Not just faster but with more love, joy, and connection.

In the Hive, not only is it better, it's faster!

WE HOLD THE HIGHEST VISION

Our thoughts shape our reality. What we send out to the universe is reflected back through our life experiences. As the saying goes, "If you want to know what you think, look at your life."

Imagine a bee sister named Sophia is struggling with her finances. She feels unsatisfied and limited in her job and is barely making ends meet. When we support Sophia, we have two possible approaches.

The first approach is to listen with an open heart but still believe that Sophia will always struggle with money—that she'll remain stuck because she doesn't have a college degree and makes poor financial decisions.

The Hive approach is to listen with an open heart and hold the highest and best vision for her. We see pure abundance surrounding her, even if we don't know how it will come into her life. We choose to see her thriving, with all her needs met and her dreams within reach. We trust that she has everything she needs to achieve her goals. We hold this vision for her, feeling grateful to witness the flow of abundance into her life. We see her living her highest dreams and desires, even if her current reality doesn't reflect that.

It doesn't serve Sophia for us to lower our energy and accept her struggles as permanent. It doesn't help her if we think she's stuck and incapable of changing her current circumstances.

Anything is possible when we hold each other in the highest and best vision.

Together, we can manifest our dreams. This is one of the most loving and powerful things we can do for one another. This approach applies to every aspect of life—whether it's finances, finding love, or achieving a life mission. When we believe in one another and hold the vision of what we're all striving to create, there's nothing we can't accomplish.

This isn't just about personal goals like money or relationships; it's about healing the planet, achieving world peace, and realizing bigger visions. By holding each other in the highest light and pursuing our lives and dreams with boldness, we can create something extraordinary.

We beelieve in you!

Bee Fact: Bee Magnetic

Bees are naturally electrostatic. As they fly, their bodies build up a positive charge, while flowers hold a negative charge. This energetic difference helps pollen leap from flower to bee— even before contact—and helps bees sense which flowers have already been visited.[20]

---

20 Clarke, D., Whitney, H., Sutton, G., & Robert, D. (2013). Detection and Learning of Floral Electric Fields by Bumblebees. Science (1880 to 2025), 340 (6128), 66–69.

BEE MAGNETIC

We have been taught one way to create, which we have used our whole lives. Some call it manifestation, creation, goal setting and tracking, or intention-setting. There are many names for it.

Instead, we bee magnetic.

When we embrace all of who we are and fully own our place in the Hive, we unlock a powerful magnetism.

This magnetism isn't something we force. It happens when we live in harmony with our true selves. It comes from two things: Alignment—being true to who we are (which the agreements help us with), and Ownership—knowing we are an important part of the Hive and honoring the importance of others. When each Bee stands fully in her presence, a deep harmony emerges, allowing us to co-create something greater than ourselves.

Imagine it's not just you setting your vision, but the whole Hive buzzing and holding that frequency, that vision.

Imagine different bees with unique gifts all working together to make your vision a reality. What would be possible?

Have a vision, a dream, a wish you want to make happen? Maybe the reason it hasn't happened yet is that it's too big for you alone.

Maybe you need the power of the Hive.

Amber Buzz: Power of Personal Hive

When I first discovered the Hive, we used this
agreement to see each other in our greatness.
We stayed connected, sharing our hopes and
dreams.

We saw each other through divorce,
And businesses closing,
My son almost dying,
Healing past sexual trauma,
Releasing mommy shame,
And moves across the country.

And with the strength of these women as a part
of my Hive,
I went to Egypt when everyone else thought I
was crazy,
I started leading my company sustainably and
profitably,
I came out of the spiritual closet with my gifts,
I finally published my book after writing it for
five years,
And I became more me.

That is the power of honoring and seeing the
bigness in one another. We gain the power to do
more than we ever could on our own.

I CHOOSE TO CROSS-POLLINATE
BECAUSE WE ARE
STRONGER TOGETHER

PART 5 ~ OUR VISION

Our Hive vision is a collective one, made up of many individual visions, including yours. We'd love to share our Bee Sisterhood visions with you and invite you to add your own. Together, we create the future.

Imagine our world living in harmony,
Each woman honoring the Holy TriniBee—
Joined in Sisterhood,
Choosing Sacred Belonging,
Using Sustainability as our compass.

Imagine knowing we are sacred and whole,
Seeing one another in our greatness,
Designed for a purpose,
Believing all of us is welcome.

Imagine knowing we belong,
No more trying to fit in or change,
Accepting ourselves
Choosing ourselves.

Imagine honoring ourselves and one another,
Honoring our yes and no,
Trusting our guidance system,
And that of our sisters.

Imagine celebrating our differences,
Seeing each other as teachers,
The light and shadow,
Mirroring it all.

Imagine if we stopped depleting ourselves and instead lived
sustainably,
And showed others they could do the same,
Letting go of control,
Living in harmony with ourselves, others and the world.

Imagine banding together,
Knowing our gifts were needed and wanted,
Holding the highest vision for one another and the world,
Unlocking bee magnetism.

Imagine the buzz of bee wisdom,
Spread woman to woman,
Community to community,
From city and country,
Across all generations
Buzzing together—

Harmony for all,
The Way of the Hive.

Nicole Buzz: My Vision

This makes me so happy that I get to share my "vision" with all of you! I share this regularly with the OG Bees, and we all smile and laugh when I allow myself to go to the place where dreams come from.

My dream is that women come together globally and decide to relate to one another in a new way. We truly embody and believe that we are all here to support one another, no matter what! The symbol of the bee is accepted worldwide as a reminder that we can all win, we can all love, and we can all heal those broken places within ourselves. I dream that through the adoption of The Hive Agreements and being in a hive together, we not only transform ourselves but also the world we live in.

Together, we rise and remember what we are capable of, that the magic of life is here, and all we need to do is connect inward to allow it to work through us. Our planet, our children, and our families are all better for the commitment we make to live a sustainable life. Together, we create a world that truly works for everyone… including the bees.

Amber Buzz: My Vision

Bee Sisterhood spreads like wildfire. Women recognize fellow bee sisters in airports, board meetings, and nursing homes. Maybe they see a bee ring or a bee bag, and with a twinkle in their eyes, they know they are part of the Hive.

Women who once saw others as rivals now embrace and celebrate one another. Differences no longer separate us. We see instead our sameness and choose to live in harmony.

Political, societal, and economic change happens because of Hive influence. The world starts shifting into a new age.

History books create a new chapter called Hive Influence and how that helped change the direction of our planet from one of depletion to one of regeneration, sustainability, and harmony.

Sacha Buzz: My Vision

My vision for the Bee Sisterhood is a global awakening of consciousness that leads to a harmonious world for all. I see this as a movement that has touched the hearts and lives of women everywhere, where collaboration over competition is the new normal, and we are hope-filled and in celebration of what we are co-creating.

I believe the Bee Sisterhood will have Hives everywhere, and in a very short amount of time, we'll see seemingly large problems—both personal and societal—solved through the innovation, generosity, and love of these individual and collective Hives in action. I believe that Bee Sisterhood will help set a new standard for women's well-being, empowerment, and happiness, which will, in turn, help create a sustainable world for all.

Jennifer Buzz: My Vision

As a hairstylist for over 20 years, I have witnessed many people unable to meet their own reflection in the mirror. "Why is that?" I asked myself. I feel like this world has been poisoned by propaganda and media. We are never enough. We *do* and *do* and *do*… and it never seems to be enough.

My vision is that each woman can look in the mirror, take a deep breath, and trust, love, and know that she belongs. When doubt clouds her mind, she chooses to say yes to herself—finding self-acceptance through sisterhood, sacred belonging, and sustainability. The Bee Sisterhood allows her to feel her wholeness. I want ALL women to know that they are never alone.

My hope is that we forget all the stories that hold us back. That we love and embrace all the parts of ourselves that seem unlovable. My prayer is that we ask for support when we need it and come to learn what we actually desire beyond what we have been told.

What's YOUR vision?

PART 6 ~
JOIN THE HIVE

Dear Bee,

We acknowledge our Hive is not complete without you.

Now that you have learned about the Way of the Hive and the Hive Agreements, this is your formal invitation to join us.

We warmly invite you to choose our Hive, become part of the Bee Sisterhood, and choose to live by our Hive agreements, perhaps inviting your sisters to do the same—embracing a life of sisterhood, sacred belonging, and sustainability as we shift the world together.

Through Bee Sisterhood, we are committed to this path, and we honor other sisterhoods and circles that are fostering connection and self-expression. Whether you choose to join our Hive or walk your own path, we celebrate your journey.

It begins and ends with choice.
You choose to know that you are sacred and whole.
You choose to belong.
You choose to honor yourself and each other.
You choose to learn from one another.
You choose to live sustainably.
You choose to cross-pollinate because
We are stronger together.

We choose, again and again
And pass along the bee wisdom to our sisters.

If you choose this experiment and join the Hive, life will never be the same.

With buzzing love,
The OG Bees
Sacha, Amber, Jennifer, and Nicole

"Buzzing In" Ceremony

The first step to join the Hive is to get buzzed in. You can join us in our buzzing ceremony online at **www.beesisterhood.com/ join**.

Once you've buzzed in, here are some additional ways to connect in the Hive:

Follow us on Social Media

Instagram **@beesisterhood**
Facebook **https://www.facebook.com/BeeSisterhood**

Take the Bee Sisterhood Sustainability Quiz

If you're looking for a simple place to start, take the Bee Sisterhood Sustainability Quiz we mentioned in Agreement #5. You'll find out where you are in and out of harmony.

This is the perfect place to start making changes to create a more sustainable life. Turn to page 169. If you would like to download and print the quiz and get support with results, head over to **www.beesisterhood.com/quiz**.

The Hive Agreements Journal

The journal is where the experiment gets real… packed with prompts, reflections, and practices drawn from *The Hive Agreements,* it takes the wisdom off the page and into your everyday life. This is how harmony spreads… one woman, one journal, one hive at a time. You can find it at **www.beesisterhood. com/book**.

Share with a Sister

Who do you know who needs or wants to walk the sustainable path?

What if your sisters, friends, and coworkers tapped into the Hive frequency?

What if we re-created a world together, led by the Hive? What would change?

Turn to page 197 and pass along this book.

Create a Hive Book Club

Create a Hive Book Club. Invite sisters you would like to invite into your hive to a book club. You can access our Hive Book Club Study Guide by going to **www.beesisterhood.com/spreadthebuzz**.

Find Your Hive

The Bee Sisterhood experiment started in 2020 and has been active ever since.

Women have been creating hives, entering this experiment, and choosing to live by the Hive Agreements. In doing so, they are exploring what becomes possible when sisterhood is intentionally nurtured.

As we witness this unfolding, a natural evolution has taken place within each hive. Something powerful is happening—a profound shift in how these women relate to one another and the stories they carry about sisterhood.

This shift is opening doors to deeper sharing, greater collaboration, and more authentic self-expression. Each woman is being invited to know herself more fully while honoring her hive sisters.

Women who never imagined themselves attending a sister circle are now hosting gatherings for others. There is no rigid blueprint for how a hive should look or function. And because of this openness, each hive is evolving in its own unique way.

The beauty of the Bee Sisterhood is that every woman brings her gifts and magic to the space. Anything is possible.

No two hives are the same—and they're not meant to be. Each holds a distinct energy and reflects the unique individuals within it. That's the magic. We get to create a hive that feels true to us.

Regardless of the shape a hive takes, one thing remains constant: the agreements and the deep honoring they invite. These shared agreements are the foundation that supports all hives in thriving.

Maybe there is a hive you are called to create. Perhaps you envision a Hive of new moms, business besties, knitting friends, local women…

Once you join our Hive, you can find a copy of our "Bee Sisterhood Circle Guidebook" with step-by-step instructions on how to hold your own bee circle at **www.beesisterhood.com/ spreadthebuzz**.

You may already have a circle or community and want to integrate the Hive Agreements.

Take it.
Use it.
Spread it.

Bee the Movement

By joining our Hive, you're now part of our movement.

Moving forward, this might look like
Continuing the experiment,
Passing along this book,
Sharing the message with others,
Offering your gifts in the Hive,
Starting a buzz book club,
Joining a Hive,
Creating your own Hive,
Going to a Bee Sisterhood retreat,
Quietly doing your sustainability work…
We're excited to hear your ideas, too!

There are so many ways to participate or create your own journey, and we trust that whatever path you choose is perfect and divinely guided. On our website, we've got lots of ways to journey with us. Head over to **www.beesisterhood.com**.

We honor your "Yes."

Thank you for saying "yes" to yourself, "yes" to the women in your life, and "yes" to us. We need you and your gifts because, together, we are a stand for harmony, and we are changing the world.

The Hive Agreements

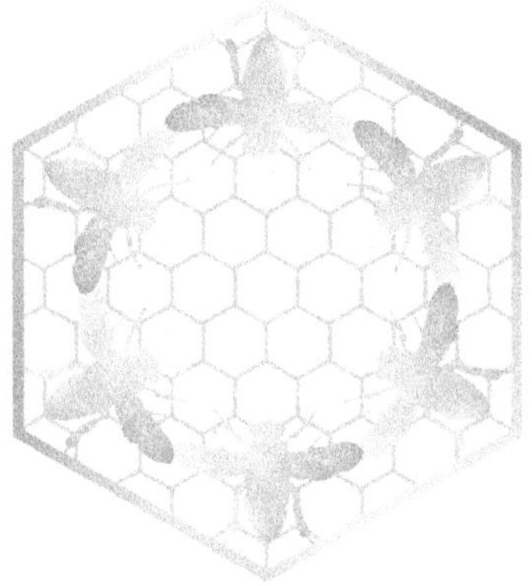

Sustainability Quiz

You can also download and print this quiz and results at
www.beesisterhood.com/quiz.

SUSTAINABILITY QUIZ

This quiz is an invitation to
Notice where you may and may not be
Living a sustainable life.
It is in the noticing we can make shifts
To come back into balance,
Our natural rhythm,
And into harmony.
Let's get started…

NAME: ____

DATE: ________________________

Each of the eight sections includes questions for you to reflect on. These are designed to help you check in with how you're feeling in that area of your life right now.

Rate yourself (from 1 to 5).

1 is Never
2 is Rarely
3 is Sometimes
4 is Usually
5 is Always

There's no right or wrong—this is a tool for awareness. Let your answers reflect how things truly feel today, not how you wish they were.

SPIRITUALITY

I feel connected to something bigger than myself. _______

I have a daily practice that strengthens my spiritual connection. _______

I believe my choices make an impact on others and the world. _______

I trust my intuition and inner wisdom. _______

I spend time in nature and feel connected to the earth. _______

I embrace change as part of life. _______

I engage in creative or expressive activities that nourish my soul. _______

I base my sense of safety on my connection with the Divine, rather than outside approval. _______

I feel a deep sense of belonging with the Divine, myself, and others. _______

I believe that my gifts and way of being are sacred by design. _______

Total Spirituality: _______

SELF

I pay attention to my feelings and energy. ________

I feel a sense of inner peace and self-acceptance. ________

I believe I am lovable. ________

I know and speak up for what I want or need ________

I take care of my basic needs. ________

I trust myself. ________

I feel safe being fully myself, without needing to perform or pretend. ________

My inner truth and outer expression is aligned. ________

I continue to learn, grow, and challenge myself. ________

I make time for myself to do things that bring me joy and are important to me. ________

Total Self: ________

BODY

I feel good in my body. _______

I nourish my body with healthy, life-giving foods every day. _______

I consciously choose what goes in and on my body. _______

I accept my body just as it is (Including weight, wrinkles, cellulite, etc.) and speak lovingly about it. _______

I have a daily practice to connect with my body (yoga, walking, meditation, breathwork, etc.). _______

I choose supportive ways to care for myself instead of self-medicating (sugar, food, caffeine, alcohol, nicotine, etc.) _______

I move my body regularly. _______

I give my body enough rest and sleep. _______

I feel connected with my pleasure & sexuality. _______

I feel connected with and allow myself to express my feelings (joy, happiness, grief, sadness, shame). _______

Total Body: _______

FAMILY

I feel at peace with my family relationships, whether we are close or not. _______

I feel free from mom guilt/family guilt. _______

I prioritize time for the family members who matter most to me. _______

I have clear boundaries with my family and take care of my own needs. _______

I trust that my family members can take care of themselves. _______

I take responsibility for what is mine and release what isn't. _______

I allow family members to be as they are without needing to fix, advise, or change them. _______

I respect each family member's choices, even when they differ from my own. _______

I express my needs and feelings openly with my family. _______

I feel my family relationships are mutual and balanced. _______

Total Family: _______

PARTNERSHIP

If in a partnership, answer the following:

I feel supported and loved by my partner. ________

I spend quality time with my partner. ________

I am honest in my relationship, even when it's hard. ________

I am comfortable expressing myself (sexually, mentally, ideas, dreams). ________

I consciously choose when I put my partner's needs before my own. ________

I let go of past arguments and move forward. ________

I feel emotionally connected in my relationship. ________

I and my partner have aligned values and goals. ________

I trust my partner to walk their own path, even when it's different from mine. ________

I release the need to be "right". ________

If not in a partnership, answer the following:

I feel happy and at peace being single. ________

I would rather be alone than settle. ________

I feel whole without a partner. ________

I trust that I am taking the right steps to find a partner (or I don't want one). ________

I believe my life is unfolding as it should, whether I have a partner or not. _______

I feel worthy of love and a good relationship. _______

I feel emotionally fulfilled in my life, regardless of my relationship status. _______

I take care of myself in the ways I would want a partner to care for me. _______

If I desire a partnership, I am creating space in my life for it. _______

I cultivate joy and fulfillment in my life outside of romantic relationships. _______

Total Partnership: _______

COMMUNITY/SISTERHOOD

I have a strong support system and feel comfortable asking for help when I need it. _______

I feel deeply seen and understood in my friendships _______

I am open to new perspectives and ideas. _______

I don't fix, give unwanted advice, or try to change other women. _______

I honor other people to make their own choices, even when it's different from mine (political, religious, parenting, sexuality, etc.) _______

I feel a sense of true belonging with other women and don't try to fit in by dimming down or holding back. _______

I speak my truth in sisterhood spaces without fear of negative consequences. _______

I celebrate the strengths and successes of other women and genuinely want the best for my sisters. _______

I trust my own path without measuring myself against others (better than or less than). _______

I choose to live in harmony with others and our world. _______

Total Community/Sisterhood: _______

PURPOSE/WORK

I feel energized from my purpose/work. _______

I love what I do. It gives me a sense of purpose and fulfillment. _______

I take breaks, eat and care for myself while working. _______

I know that who I am is more than what I do. _______

I have a work/life balance. _______

I set boundaries at work to protect my time and energy. _______

I no longer over-give or work from a place of depletion. _______

I only say yes to what is truly mine to do. _______

I share my gifts and wisdom with others. _______

I am valued and respected in my position at home or work. _______

Total Purpose/Work: _______

FINANCES

I feel abundant. ________

I trust my financial decisions. ________

My household has enough money to meet our needs without debt. ________

I feel secure and excited about my financial future. ________

It always feels like I have enough money. ________

I find it easy to receive (money, financial support, gifts, etc.) ________

My self-worth is not tied to my financial success. ________

My financial choices reflect my values. ________

I save and invest for my future. ________

I give freely knowing there is more than enough. ________

Total Finances: ________

How to Fill In Your Hive Sustainability Wheel

The wheel is divided into pie-shaped sections, each representing a different area of your life—such as health, relationships, career, spirituality, and more.

Color in each section with your score. For 10 points, you'd color in 1/5 the section. For 25 points, 1/2 the section. For 50 points, you'd fully color it in, etc.

The goal of this is to put a time stamp to see where we are at, where we get to focus our attention and see places we are living unsustainably and may be out of harmony.

If you'd like to do this quiz online, head over to **beesisterhood.com/quiz** and see what area you're called to bring into harmony at this time.

HIVE SUSTAINABILITY WHEEL

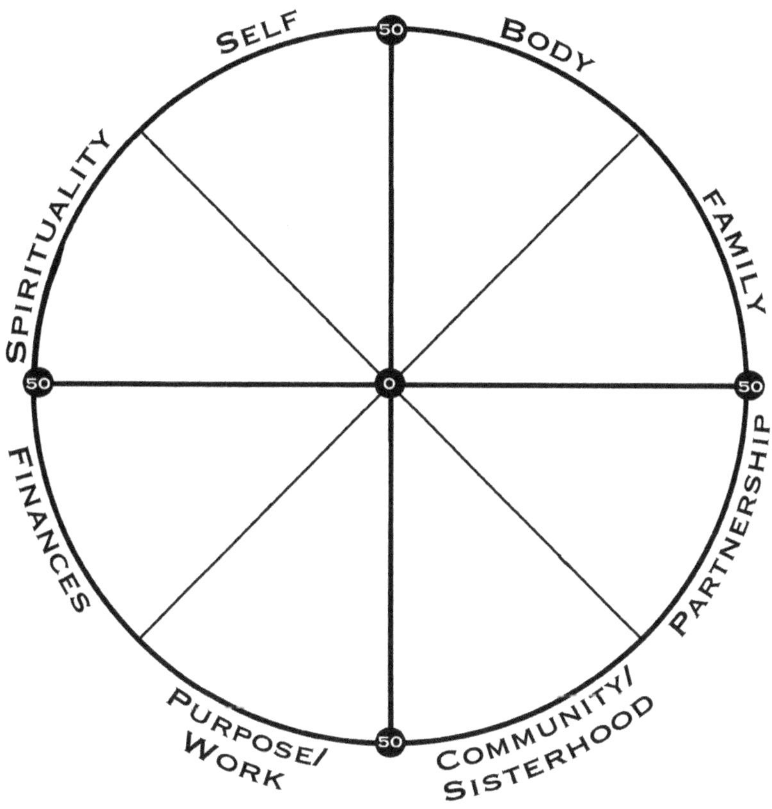

Spirituality______   Partnership______

Self______   Community/Sisterhood______

Body______   Purpose/Work______

Family______   Finances______

Acknowledgments

To the bees, thank you for sharing your wisdom and bringing us together.

To Anahita Ahura, Aaron Ahura, Brian Walsh, and Elizabeth Walsh, thank you for holding sacred space and bringing us together for the Bee Sisterhood to be born.

To Darcy Meehan, you've been our honorary bee sister before there was such a thing. Water baptisms at Bee Cave and all.

To our first bee sisters from our first retreat, this initial hive showed us the potency of this movement.

To our early readers, thank you for your honest feedback.

To the land where we wrote and developed the Hive Agreements: Big Island Hawai'i, Sacred Ground, California, Mendocino, California, San Clemente, California, Blissful Hill Retreat in Bee Cave, Texas, thank you for holding us.

To Bee Sister and Book Bee Jane Scott Ashley, thank you for helping weave the message of the Hive and four authors into a cohesive message to be buzzed around the world. Thank you for creating the book design and layout, for understanding the vision of the Hive Agreements, and for bringing it to life.

To our personal hives...

Amber

To Tony, my partner and best friend, thank you for holding this vision with me.

To my sons Sage and Bodhi, my vision of a world in harmony is for you.

To Mom and Dad, Mom and Dad you, you're the best support team ever.

To my brothers and sisters Jessica, Mike, Noah, Heather, Mariea, Kurt, Erik, Lacey, Hannah, Matt, Frankie, and Natalie, I'm glad our hive combined.

To Suzy, Wendy, Lou, Shiloh, the Oracle of 8, and my Kona Hive, Elli and Crystal... thank you for living and walking this vision with me.

To Unleashers, when I picture Bee Sisterhood, I see your faces.

To Sacha, Nicole, Jennifer, you are my home, my hive, my heart.

Sacha

Thank you to the Bees—past, present, and future. Your presence, wisdom, and magic have been one of the biggest surprises of my life so far.

To my daughters, Isis and Aria. My greatest teachers and deepest motivators to do my own healing, to model empowerment for you, and help create a world you deserve.

To my beloved husband, Steve, and our son, Meric, the bees brought us together (in Bee Cave) for the most profound, heart-opening experience.

To all of the family, friends, and community who supported this body of work, you are so loved and appreciated.

To my Bee Sisters, Jennifer, Amber, and Nicole: Your love and friendship have and continue to bless every part of my life. Thank you for saying YES to me, and us and the Bee Sisterhood.

Jennifer

Thank you to my partner, Scott, for sticking with the changes and flow that comes with transformation.

To my son Ethan, for always catching me when I'm "broken." Being a single mother at a young age has taught my son to know when to be the strong backbone when another is breaking down.

To my parents, who have always been my biggest cheerleaders. Thank you for creating a loving space to grow and express fully while being accepted. Thank you.

I thank the universe, God, Goddess, and Big BEE in the sky for having our back through this whole process.

Nicole

Thank you to Brian Fox, for being a grounding force in my life, so I can manifest my dreams—you are my biggest bee supporter.

To Gavin, Samantha, and Brianna, you are truly the greatest achievement in this lifetime, and I am beyond grateful to be your mom.

To my mom, dad, and sister Pam, thank you for always believing in me even when I did not believe in myself.

To Janea, Charlene, and Elizabeth, your friendship and sisterhood have been supportive throughout this entire process.

To all my girls Sarah, Lily, Rachel, Marty, Erica, Jen & Michelle—I love you all so much and am grateful for our hive.

Mandy, my oldest friend, I miss you every day and know you are here with me.

Lastly, Amber, Sacha, and Jennifer, there are no words to express the gratitude in my heart for our hive and what it has done in my life.

The OG Bees. Also known as…

Sacha Sterling Arpaia

Sacha Sterling Arpaia is the founder of The Devotion, a global sanctuary of spiritual empowerment where women harmonize with the frequency of their vision, embody spiritual security, and live as devoted co-creators.

A Master Empowerment Coach since 2010 and host of a top-ranking podcast, Sacha has reached hundreds of thousands of women worldwide, guiding them to release fear-based patterns, heal spiritual wounds, and step into full energetic sovereignty.

Her signature frameworks, Vision Mantra™ and Spiritual Attachment Style™, blend mysticism with neuroscience to support women in manifesting with confidence and certainty.

Sacha lives with her husband and three children on their Texas homestead. She believes Heaven on Earth is not a faraway place, but a frequency we can choose, embody, and practice together, raising the consciousness of humanity and co-creating a more harmonious world.

Amber Kuileimailani Bonnici

International Bestselling Author, Award Winning Artist, and Founder of Woman Unleashed, a community dedicated to helping women connect to their creative spirit to feel on purpose, happy, and free. Amber hosts the Woman Unleashed Online Retreat, which has drawn more than 200,000 women since it first began.

Her book *Creativity Unleashed: A Woman's Guide to Unlock Flow and Finish Your Creative Work* was an International Bestseller and supports women to get creating. Her artwork has been featured at the United Nations Commission on the Status of Women.

She lives in Kailua Kona, Hawai'i, with her husband, Tony, and is the proud mama of her two sons, Sage and Bodhi.

Jennifer Brown

Jennifer's path is one of self-love and self-acceptance. At the young age of 19, she was married, divorced, and had a son. She is a force of non-judgmental authentic power. As the priestess of permission, Jennifer, also known as Feather to her friends, expresses her emotions freely.

She has been an independent Hairstylist for over 20 years. She creates a Hairstyle for your lifestyle while truly listening to each client. Jennifer is the inventor of the Ritual Haircut, which allows clients to release unwanted baggage and step into their full potential.

She is a self-love coach who uses the true essence of colors and clothes to guide women on the path to full self-acceptance. She has guided hundreds of women to own and embrace their own beauty. She has taught this Self-adornment work around the world.

Jennifer's favorite place is in transformational spaces. She offers bodywork as a healing modality. She dances like she knows life is worth living. She lives in Southern California and is looking for places to explore.

Nicole Fox

Nicole Fox is a force in the field of functional medicine, with over 24 years of experience transforming the way healthcare is delivered and understood. A trusted advisor and collaborator to many of the top thought leaders in integrative and personalized medicine, Nicole blends science, soul, and strategy in everything she does.

Holding a Master's degree in Spiritual Psychology, she has a rare gift for bridging clinical expertise with the deeper realms of healing. Nicole is the co-founder of a thriving integrative family practice in Temecula, California, and the founder of a consulting firm that empowers visionary businesses and educational platforms to integrate the healing arts and spiritual intelligence into their work.

As Chief Operating Officer of the Personalized Lifestyle Medicine Institute, Nicole brings cutting-edge education in functional, integrative, and personalized medicine to hundreds of thousands of healthcare professionals across the globe—helping to shift the paradigm of modern healthcare.

She lives in San Clemente, California, with her husband, twins, and three dogs. Whether at home, working, or facilitating sister circles, Nicole leads with heart and a bold commitment to healing at every level.

SPREAD THE BUZZ

Dear Bee Sister,

A fellow Bee Sister loves you and believes our hive is not complete without you.

This book is an invitation to remember the wisdom of the hive and the power of women who work together. By accepting this book, you are invited to step into a community committed to living these sacred agreements:

1. We are Sacred and Whole

We do not see each other as small. We see each other as whole. We hold each other in our highest possibility, even if it doesn't look that way.

2. We All Belong

We accept and love all of you. This is a place where we know each of us already belongs, just as we are. There is nothing we need to do.

3. We Honor Ourselves and Each Other

We believe that all women have a divine guidance system, and we honor how it expresses itself. We do not try to fix each other. We do not gossip. We take up our space.

4. We Learn from Each Other

We get to own, love, and accept all aspects of ourselves in what we see reflected in each of our Hive sisters. We welcome all of each other: the light as well as the shadow.

5. We Live Sustainably

We choose to live in harmony with ourselves, then with others and our world. We no longer create from depletion. We trust ourselves to know what is and is not ours to do.

6. We are Stronger Together

We don't need to do things alone. No bee left behind. We hold your dreams and stories as sacred. We see your desires magnetizing to you right now. We are meant to cross-pollinate.

If these words resonate with you, receive this book and the buzz within these pages.

The hive grows through women like you. If this book touches your heart, pass it forward to another woman you love and invite her to add her name to this lineage.

With buzzing love,

The OG Bees

This book has traveled through these Bee Sisters:

Received by: ____

Gifted by: ____

Date: ____

Received by: ____

Gifted by: ____

Date: ____

Received by: ____

Gifted by: ____

Date: ____

Received by: ____

Gifted by: ____

Date: ____

Received by: ____

Gifted by: ____

Date: ____

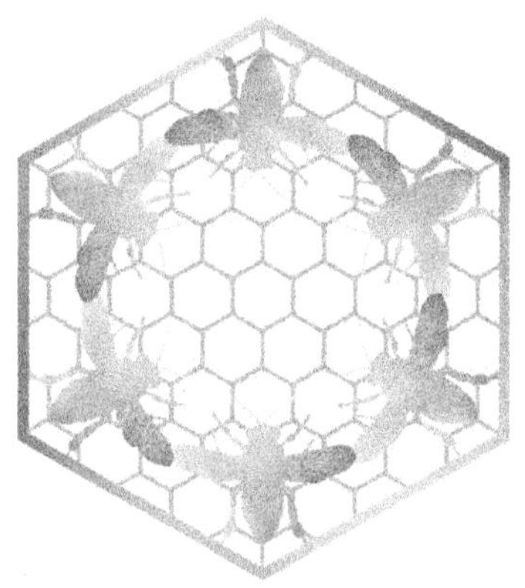

www.ingramcontent.com/pod-product-compliance
Lightning Source LLC
Chambersburg PA
CBHW041312120726
48005CB00014B/1978